D1707494

TALES OF THE PHILIPPINES - IN THE EARLY 1900'S

By

SIMON BOLIVAR BUCKNER, JR.

Lieutenant Buckner with Philippine Natives

TALES OF THE PHILIPPINES - IN THE EARLY 1900'S

By

SIMON BOLIVAR BUCKNER, JR.

BUCKNER'S STORIES AND PHOTOGRAPHS ARE ABOUT THE PHILIPPINES AT THE BEGINNING OF THE 1900'S WHEN IT WAS EXOTIC, DANGEROUS, ENTHRALLING AND EXCITING.

I wish to acknowledge the enthusiastic help from family friend, Tully Moss III, who lives and works in the Philippines. We worked together to write a Preface which would hopefully turn the precious manuscript and album my father willed to me into a fascinating, historical, and relevant book.

– William C. Buckner.

PREFACE

This is a trip back in time. It is a trip back to a time of unspoiled beauty. It is a trip by a young man to a world that no longer exists…and yet, a world that, in fundamental ways, lives on.

The young man who traveled that world was my father, Lieutenant Simon Bolivar Buckner, Jr. The world that he ventured in was that of the Philippines at the beginning of the 1900s.

When he first went to the Philippines, Lieutenant Buckner was in his early twenties. He had graduated from West Point in 1908, after which he spent two years in Texas on Mexican border patrol. It was there he learned a little Spanish, which would prove useful when he went to the Philippine Islands in 1910: the Philippines had been a Spanish colony for over three hundred years, only little more than a decade before Lieutenant Buckner's first trip there.

This book contains about eighty tales which average about two pages each, so this book is easy to read. These are stories of an adventurous young man who had a keen eye for beauty and who was an astute observer of human behavior. You will read about the considerable dangers that confronted travelers to the Philippines: headhunters, hostility toward American soldiers, and life threatening diseases such as cholera and dengue. None of this seems to have phased Lieutenant Buckner. For example, about half way through the book, you will read how he had heard so much about the wildness of the people in the southern part of the Philippines that "I could not resist a desire to go there and disappear for a few days in its jungles" – despite the fact that two Americans had been killed there a mere month-and-a-half previously.

Lieutenant Buckner's ability to write about his adventures was enhanced by the fact that, at the time, he was a bachelor with three months of unspent leave. His travels around the Philippines were facilitated by his father, the ex-governor of Kentucky, who had shipped him a twenty-five foot motor launch, which enables Lieutenant Buckner to travel among various Philippine islands.

THE PHILIPPINE ISLANDS

The Philippines is an archipelago of 7,107 islands stretching over 1,100 miles (1,800 kilometers) along a northwest-southeast axis in the Sulu, Celebes, Philippine, and South China Seas. These islands have been grouped into three divisions: Luzon, in the north (which includes several small-to-modest-sized islands as well as a large island that is also named Luzon): the Visages in the central part of the country, and Mindanao in the south. You will read how Lieutenant Buckner traveled virtually the full length of the Philippines – from Manila (in the north) to the Visayas (in the middle of the country) to Jolo, Mindanao (in the southern part of the Philippines).

Colonial Era

The Philippines was a Spanish colony for over three hundred years, from 1565 to 1898. Prior to the Spanish, the Philippine archipelago had not been unified under one political state. Smaller naval entities had ruled individual villages. Colonization commenced with the arrival of Miguel Lopez de Legazpi, who established the first European settlements in Cebu (in the Visayas) from 1565 to 1821 and subsequently was governed from Madrid after the Mexican War of Independence.

The Spanish-American War of 1898 resulted in the Philippine archipelago being ceded to the United States. Almost immediately there was a revolt against American rule, and you will read in Lieutenant Buckner's writings how virulent anti-American sentiments were still prevalent in some parts of the Philippines where he traveled.

Revolts against the U.S. rule were suppressed, and the Philippines in subsequent decades has had a mostly friendly relationship with the United States.

The U.S. maintained a significant military presence in the Philippines during the first half of the twentieth century. General Douglas MacArthur commanded U.S. (and Philippine) forces for a number of years. Serving in the Philippines under General MacArthur during pre-World War II days was Dwight Eisenhower (who remarked that it was under MacArthur that he learned "drama"). The connection between the U.S. Army and the Philippines continues to this day, as there have been nearly 80 Filipino graduates of West Point.

Independence

Plans for granting independence to the Philippines were delayed by the onset of World War II, during which over a million Filipinos – six percent of the population – were killed. On July 4, 1946, the Philippines achieved independence, becoming a constitutional republic with a popularly elected president, senate and house of representatives.

Lingering resentments against colonial rule on occasion flare up. In the early 1990s, the Philippine government revoked the right of the U.S. military to use Subic Naval Base, and the current Philippine President, Rodrigo Duterte, has been vigorously anti-American in many of his statements. But ties between the two countries remain deep. There are millions of Filipinos living in the United States, and it is the dream of millions more to migrate to the U.S. In the Philippines itself, the largest private employer in the country, Convergys, is an American company, and over a million Filipinos work in the outsourcing industry, which primarily serves the U.S. market. American culture – movies, music, and television shows – are prevalent in the Philippines.

READING TALES OF THE PHILIPPINES

I have not edited Lieutenant Buckner's language: what you will read is entirely his own. At certain points in the book, some may interpret that language as the condescension of a colonialist, and that may grate on modern sensibilities. But those who can get beyond the use of words such as "boy" (for male household help) and "heathen" (for non-Christian Filipinos) will find Lieutenant Buckner to be anything but arrogant and condescending. Instead, you will see that he was a keen, unbiased observer of human behavior, and in his own way showed that he cared about doing what was right, regardless of an individual's nationality.

His language is that of the early twentieth century. It tends to be understated and at time formal, and it lacks the punch and loud directness of twenty-first century American English. But patient readers will marvel at what they find: a military man with a poet's eye for natural beauty, and anthropologist's disciplined, insightful observations of human behavior, and a humorist's ability to poke fun at the antics and foolhardy behavior of Westerners and Filipinos alike.

Those who read this account even more carefully may discern in Lieutenant Buckner those qualities that eventually enabled him to rise in the ranks and become General Buckner. You will see in these stories of his Philippine adventures how he was displaying, at a relatively young age, an exceptional degree of bravery and independent thinking and an exceptional ability to read situations and people, to bring order where there was chaos, and to think quickly it saves lives.

And now for Lieutenant Buckner's adventures in the land of the Philippines....the adventures of a lifetime.

SUMMARY OF CHAPTERS

LIST OF ILLUSTRATIONS

CHAPTER I

Exile or Paradise - Aces and Tens - Honolulu - Pajamas – Guam.

Two years in the Philippines! There were few members of the regiment in whom this order awakened exactly the same emotions. This I gathered as I strolled about on deck and picked up scraps from the hum of conversation to which the sailing of a transport seems always to give impetus.

"Yes, he was a splendid officer but the tropics got him. It gets a lot of them," I heard one of the major's remark. I paused a moment to learn just how the tropics "gets them," but the conversation drifted to the beauties of Pagsanjan, the gorgeous sunsets over Mariveles mountain, and the twenty varieties of orchids which had blossomed on the Colonel's *azotea* in Zamboanga, and my curiosity was left unsatisfied until a later day. In another group, a tall, spare captain, with steel-blue eyes and sun-tanned, leathery face was stretched comfortably in a steamer chair.

"Yes," he said, "it somehow gets into your blood. When you have once lived in the East and been a part of it, you will always come back. The first whiff of the pungent smoke of burning bamboo will banish every unpleasant memory of the past, and with it, every worry about the future; and you can live as a real gentleman lived before the Yankees took our slaves away. I venture to say that in the Philippines there are more beautiful ---".

At this point the stocky, florid officer next to him threw his cigar stump overboard with an impatient gesture and broke in: "Yes, there you go with your call of the East stuff about this damned hole where we are about to bury ourselves for the next two years. You will always come back, there's no doubt about that, if you stay in the army long enough. For that matter, if you step into a grave you can feel equally sure of returning. Not an opera, not a show, not a chorus, not a decent restaurant, not a morning paper, not a damned thing. Who wants to smell bamboo smoke or dead fish or coconut oil or any other oriental stink? Who wants to get the dengue fever or the dhobi itch or the amoebic dysentery? Who wants to sit around in a place where there is so little going on that you have to amuse yourselves by betting which finger of your leprous neighbor will drop off next? A hell of a country for a white man!"

During the next two days the bridge friends began to assemble and to enslave that unfortunate victim whose services are so often called upon "to make a fourth." Meanwhile, below deck in a secluded corner, little red, white and blue objects began to follow straight and full houses around the table. Never was there a time more suitable to the inveterate poker-player than a month's voyage on the ocean. And so, the little group befogged the atmosphere of their tiny room with tobacco smoke, blessed the Goddess of Fortune for the third seven, or grieved over the undue confidence which they had bestowed upon aces and tens.

In this way, last month's pay, this month's pay and sometimes even next month's pay ebbed and flowed. Thus, throughout the month, the game moved happily along, marred only by the occasional presence of that infernal nuisance, the "rail bird," the idiot who strolls around the table, peers into your hand, and gives you an obviously congratulatory grin and nod when you catch the card you have been hoping for.

About the third day out, a stiff breeze sprang up, and the old Sherman began to roll and pitch through a district of migratory aquatic mountains. Long, ghastly faces of a color suggestive of lavender appeared from time to time on deck and then disappeared into the staterooms below. The regimental band struggled out on deck at the usual hour for a cheering concert, but the result was pitiable. Imagine the joys of blowing a horn while sea-sick.

A few of us who were still unshaken amused ourselves, by watching the efforts of the trombone player. At each rise of the ship's bow, the muscles of his arm involuntarily contracted and a high note would invariably result. Then, in the long downward plunge which followed, the trombone slide would automatically stretch out to its fullest extent, and then utter a deep bass gasp. After four such gasps, the instrument lay on deck deserted by its guardian. Three more members of the band were soon similarly taken, and the concert ended.

Toward the end of the week, the damp, cutting wind subsided into a summer breeze, and the turbulent, gray ocean brightened into sparkling blue which danced and glistened in the sun. Little flocks of flying fish began to rise under our bow, skim along above the waves, and fall back with a splash into their element. At length, we could see land - mountains lightly clad in delicate green, tinted with the red of volcanic earth, and dimpled with ancient craters. Above them, against a sky of luminous blue, were masses of those big, white clouds which hang over tropical islands. As we neared, we could see a long line of breakers lashing themselves into froth against the outer barrier of coral, and then a glistening beach of white sand fringed with the rich green of luxuriant foliage. From the deep indigo of the outer ocean, we glided past the foaming breakers and into the pale green waters of Honolulu harbor.

I went below to make an inspection of the troop deck and heard two soldiers excitedly discussing the possibilities of the next two days. "Ain't you never seen pictures of 'em?" said the taller of the two, they are pretty to look at, and don't wear nothin' but little

Kanaka Boys who dived for our Pennies

bunches of grass tied around their waists with a string, and they set around and play music and dance the hula-hula all day." My inspection led me out of earshot, and I returned to the upper deck, where in a few minutes I was throwing pennies to be dived for by the "Kanaka" boys who swam out from the dock to meet the transport.

The gang plank was scarcely lowered, when we began to file out on shore and spend hours, all too short, enjoying the charms of an island which has been called "Pearl of the Ocean," "Paradise of the Pacific," and "Fairyland of the Sea." Whatever may be the time of year, Honolulu has the climate of perpetual spring; its skies are clear and brilliant, its foliage full of the freshness of early June, its flowers are always in full bloom and its soft breezes laden with their perfume. Who can stand on the Pali, that gigantic amphitheater of massive rock, and look unmoved upon all that nature has laid before him? Below, are rolling foot-hills of red soil shading into rose-color and brown and cut into delicate patterns by little lines and patches of vegetation. Beyond these is the pale lettuce-shade of rice fields, the sweep, of a shining beach, the luminous green of clear water over shoals of golden sand, and then the long breakers rolling in from the ocean and leaping in white spray over the outer reef. The rugged grandeur of massive form, the balanced symmetry exquisite pattern, the richness of contrasted color and the harmony of blended tints - all are there beneath a sky which enhances their beauty with ever-changing light.

It is hard to believe that scarcely more than a century and a half ago white men had never trod upon the island of Oahu, and now they were masters of a fast-vanishing people. It was as late as 1778 that Cook's expedition first found the Hawaiians, a race living in the joys of primitive simplicity. They loved the beauties of nature, wove the flowers of their native land into garlands for their hair, worshiped their gods in happiness, killed each other by way of diversion, and splattered Cook's brains with a club.

Many songs have been written about dreamy-eyed Hawaiian maidens dancing the hula-hula Waikiki beach, accompanied by seductive music from the ukulele and steel guitar. Having heard these songs, it is not entirely without certain vague Utopian imaginings that most of us drifted out to Waikiki on our first afternoon. Perhaps many began by being disappointed when they found that the only truly primitive exhibitions there were the antics of some tourists who imagined themselves suddenly transformed by the atmosphere of the tropics.

But disappointment soon gave way to delight when we caught sight of the natives on their surf boards. With these, the natives swim out about a mile into the breakers, and when a suitable wave comes along, mount to a standing position on the board, and poised on the shoreward slant of the wave, come gliding in to the beach, the curling crest of the breakers only a few feet behind them. I do not recall with any great degree of pride my first attempt to emulate them.

Supper time found me with a classmate in the dining room of the Moana. We had heard that poi, made from the root of the taro, was the national dish of the Hawaiians, it being served in the various forms of "one finger" poi, "two finger poi" or "three-finger poi," according to its stickiness and the degree of skill manifested by the consumer. We called the waiter, and with the air of old inhabitants, remarked that we would start dinner with a little poi. He produced this, and after watching us taste it, straightaway removed it and presented us with the bill-of-fare. If you have any curiosity regarding poi, dissolve a cake of yeast in buttermilk, stir in enough mud to make a paste, and watch someone else taste it.

As we sat by the window watching the soft crayon tints fade from the evening sky and listened to the muffled roar of distant breakers, the room slowly began to fill. Officers and ladies of our regiment, and from the Honolulu garrison, came strolling in. The bright colors worn by the latter were in vivid contrast to the freshly-starched white uniforms of their escorts. Most of the ladies wore flowers. There is some quality in the atmosphere of Honolulu which seems to inspire us with a desire to give flowers, to seek someone to whom our flowers will bring happiness - a dangerous place for a young bachelor.

Dinner over, the tables were removed, and an Hawaiian orchestra played, or rather sang, for more than half of their music came from their voices, which blended beautifully with the ukuleles and guitars. Then we danced - or was it a dream in which we floated about like bubbles in a perfumed atmosphere? Was there really a moon-lit pier, the sound of distant music, a pair of dark eyes, a few eager whispers and a moment of rapture? If not, we must go back, for Honolulu was created to make love in.

All too soon, we found ourselves once more on the Sherman. Our necks were laden with leis, farewell garlands of flowers, and as the transport slowly moved off, the Royal Hawaiian band accompanied the clear, mellow voice of a woman who, with her arms stretched out toward us sang "Aloha Oe." In a few minutes the last *kanaka* had dived from our bridge and we were off on another lap of our journey.

We were headed for Guam, over a twenty-five hundred mile stretch of mirror-like water, with neither land nor ship to break the horizon-line during the eleven days of our voyage.

Despite all this, events were aplenty. Boxing and wrestling matches among the soldiers, flirtations, bridge games, a minstrel show, fights between small boys who had thrown each other's toys overboard, the reading of melodramatic novels, concerts by the band, practical jokes of a most diabolical character, dances on deck, vaccination against smallpox, charades, the formation of a glee club, violent protests against the glee club's activities during the siesta hour, and pajama parties on deck by moonlight.

It seems to be a strange sartorial phenomenon, that in whatever part of the world you may be, when a ship sails into tropical waters, pajamas invariably find their way on deck. Formality may reign supreme at dinner and white uniforms and evening dresses may be essential, but when the lights are turned off and a soft tropical breeze fans the moon-lit deck, the pajama will out. It peeps from beneath a bath robe, while its feminine counterpart is covered only by a prettily embroidered kimono.

The palm trees of Guam were a welcome sight, and as we entered the harbor, I recalled the story of its capture by part of Admiral Dewey's fleet during our war with Spain. As to whether the circumstances of its surrender constituted a joke at the expense of the Spanish garrison or the American fleet, authorities in these two countries differ. The Spanish governor of Guam, not being connected by cable with the rest of the world, was enjoying the peaceful pursuit of tropical happiness, totally unaware of the fact that his country was at war, when the roar of cannon announced the arrival of Dewey's fleet. The Governor was a man most punctilious in matters of courtesy, and while the Americans' guns still thundered, sent a launch to our flagship with the message that though he felt highly honored, he deeply regretted he did not have sufficient powder to return the salute.

We did not go ashore that evening, but a number of the naval and marine officers and their families came out to the transport. We all enjoyed a dance on deck. It was almost pathetic to see the eagerness with which our visitors seized the antiquated papers and magazines which we had on board. Aside from the occasional cablegram they received, the only glimpse they had of the outside world was this transport which comes once a month and stays less than twenty-four hours.

Next morning we were up with the sun, and as an eye-opener, Johnson and I decided to take a swim. The smooth, unrippled surface of the water invited a plunge, so we dived from the upper deck like a couple of big bull-frogs, and started swimming around the ship. As we approached the stern, we looked up and saw two sailors on deck, looking intently into the water. One had a .22 rifle, and as we approached, the other pointed to a spot about fifty yards in front of us and remarked, "There they are, let 'em have it." Then, catching sight of us, he added in a lazy drawl "Say, we've been shootin' at a school of sharks, nine of 'em altogether, and I wouldn't advise you all to go too close to 'em. They tell me that some of 'em bite, and ----" The last of his remark was lost in the distance. Two white streaks started for the gangway, which hung from the middle of the opposite side of the ship. Several times, I was certain that I felt my stomach being bitten out, and when we finally pulled ourselves out of the water, I saw Johnny take inventory of his left leg with an expression of surprised satisfaction which indicated beyond doubt that he had not expected to find it there.

After breakfast, a little launch put out from Piti for the purpose of taking us ashore. As it carried us along through the narrow channel in the white coral bottom of the harbor, we could see schools of the brightly-colored fish which inhabit tropical waters, darting to cover at our approach. Beyond this coral bank, lay the clean, white sand of the beach, then a low, palm-covered strip, back of which rose a table-land cut by heavily-forested valleys which were broken by several peaks of volcanic origin.

As we crossed the inner harbor, we missed the hundreds of beautiful painted *praus* with their graceful triangular sails which *Pigafetta* so admired when the island was discovered by Magellan. In fact, there was scarcely a boat to be seen, the native having apparently lost his former love for life on the ocean. It is not unreasonable to attribute this change in his tastes to the large infusion of foreign blood which took place during the early Spanish regime. This was due partly to the importation of *Tagalogs* from the Philippines, but perhaps to a greater extent to the fact that great numbers of the men were killed off by the Spanish and Mexican garrisons, and their women appropriated by the soldiers. The result has been that while the old Chamorro still forms the basis of the population, the race which has evolved is scarcely distinguishable in appearance from the Filipino.

Behind the landing place at Piti, we found a large proportion of the island's means of transportation drawn up ready to take us to *Agaña*, the principal town some five miles up the shore. There were ox-carts with solid wooden wheels, a sulky drawn by a cow, and numerous nondescript conveyances drawn by native ponies. Just how all these vehicles got there that morning, it is hard to conjecture, for the drivers of the first two into which Johnson and I climbed were wholly unable to get under way. Next we tried a dilapidated surrey of ancient pattern, our hopes being based upon the fact that the horse appeared to lack force of character and the driver to possess considerable determination. With great care, the latter led our steed into the middle of the road and pointed him in the right direction; then mounting to his seat, he gave the whip a flourish, and off we started - not forward, but backward. A second attempt was more successful. The animal was led until he broke into a trot, and our native, after making a flying hop for the seat, caught up the reins and looked around at us for approbation. This, we would undoubtedly have given, had not another retro-

grade movement of the horse backed us over a steep bank into a bread fruit tree, happily with no damage except to the harness, which we soon repaired and proceeded without further mishap.

The road to *Agaña* was shaded by rows of tall coconut palms, each with little steps cut in its trunk for convenience in gathering its fruit or the cider-like sap from which *tuba* is made. Native houses, usually of wood, were scattered all along the way, each set on stilts and thatched with palm leaves. Naked children smiled and waved to us as we passed, women squatted in their doorways smoking long, home-made cigars, or busied themselves drying corn or copra by the roadside on mats of their own weaving. Here and there, through breaks in the palm-groves, we could see tiny rice fields whose muddy soil was being stirred with crude plows, each drawn by a *carabao*. There was work going on, little odd jobs here and there, but not enough to detract from the air of care-free happiness in which these islanders appear to dwell. Groups of them were gathered in the cool shadow of the palm trees, the brown arms and legs of women protruding from beneath brightly-colored calico, the men bare-footed and wearing more or less clothing. Those who wore more, radiated pride and perspiration; those with less, comfort and envy.

Upon entering *Agaña*, what impressed me most, and surprised me not a little was its scrupulous cleanliness. This at once led me to place the Chamorro in a position high above his kindred races. Only a few minutes later, however, I saw a native come rushing out of his house and become active with a broom in response to the sharp call of a marine soldier who was poking in the corner of his yard with a stick and holding his nose. I then realized that it was the naval government which had banished dirt from *Agaña*, and the Chamorro dived unceremoni-ously to a place among his fellows.

The Gallaghers arrived in a Bull Cart

The Governor gas giving a lunch-eon and had invited a number of our fellow-passengers to his "palace," but since his hospitality was limited by his accommodations and his guests invited from the higher-ranking end of the list, the younger lieutenants could not be included. Consequently, we began to collect at "The Club," a general gather-ing-place for the white population of the island. Here, we sat on the shady verandah facing the open plaza in front of the marine barracks, and enjoyed long, cool drinks while awaiting the arrival of the others. Before long, the Gallaghers rolled up in a bull-cart, and after nearly two hours, Tucker, Hollingsworth and George Simpson brought up the rear of the procession. Simpson seemed very much out of breath, a condition which the others attributed to the fact that he was the self-appointed linguist of the group, and in his efforts to reach the club, had already conducted them on a tour including the palace, the ice plant and host of the points of interest in and about *Agaña*.

Before long, the regimental baseball team arrived, and the marines had their monthly big game on the plaza - this game which follows the American wherever he goes, and which the natives so soon learn to relish with almost equal enthusiasm. Wherever I have seen it played, it has seemed part of the ethics of the game that it be played in English. Often I have watched games between Tagalogs, Igorots, and Chamorros who spoke no other word of English, and heard the familiar sounds of "faol bol" and "estrika one" when occasion demanded them. In Cebú, when a Visayan team was coming to the bat, I heard their captain solemnly announce: "Pablo of the bat, Juan of the deck, Jesus of the hole."

At luncheon we had sufficiently recovered from our poi experience to clamor again for some form of non-poisonous food which was distinctly native. The waiter spoke fairly good English, but the terms "distinctly native" and "characteristically Chamorran" put him into a state of mental depression. In turn, each of us tried him, then we all tried him at once, following which we relapsed into exhausted silence. After solemnly regarding us for several minutes, an idea which had been filtering through the crevices suddenly struck his brain. His face brightened, and with the remark, "bombashoot," he disappeared, leaving us in a state of perplexity. A few minutes later, be returned with a mysterious-looking salad, which we found to be delicious. "Bombashoot" it was, the tender, asparagus-like shoots of young bamboo.

Before returning to the Sherman, we mingled for a while among the marine officers of the garrison. At first we were inclined to pity them in their isolation, but they almost persuaded us to envy them before we left. It could never be said that they were not making the best of it. They rode and hiked around the island, they danced and had concerts at night, they sailed, swam, caught sharks beyond the reef, hunted deer and wild boar, played poker, and withal did enough work to keep their troops interested and in good condition and themselves from going to seed.

We took with us mail for "the States" which was to travel via Manila to San Francisco, and with baskets of fresh tropical fruits, boarded our little launch at Piti. A few hours later we had seen our last of Guam, which, small and isolated as it may be, is nevertheless an important relay-station for the trans-Pacific cable, and a vital link in the chain of strategic naval bases between America and the Orient.

CHAPTER II

San Bernardino - Cholera - Pulijanes in Samar - The Fire Cure.

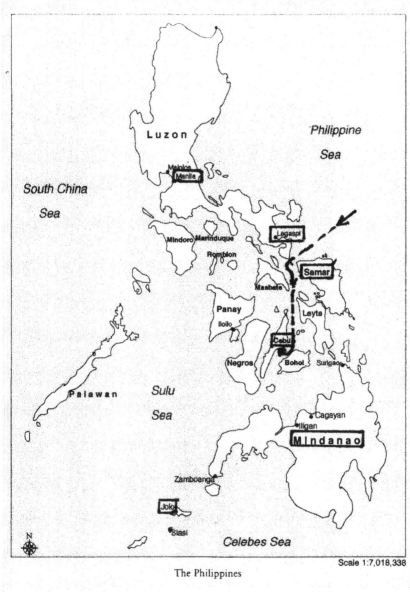

The Philippines

Scale 1:7,018,338

We had reached San Bernardino Strait. At last we were in the Philippines! To the north of us was Luzon, with its quaint old city of Manila, its lakes and fertile plains, its volcanoes, its sky and almost inaccessible pygmy Negritos, its wealth of hardwood forests and its head-hunting mountain tribes. To the south lay the Island of Samar, whose rugged mountain tops rose high into the clouds? I had heard a hundred tales of hardship and bloodshed in subduing its warlike Pulajanes, tales of mantraps which drove spears through the luckless soldiers who stepped within their reach, of pitfalls lined with spikes, of prisoners buried alive, or bound naked and smeared with honey until the flesh was eaten from their bones by ants. But now that our troops had forced its mountain jungles, its inhabitants were happy and prospering under the government which they had at first so mistrusted.

The sea was calm, broken only by the splash of porpoises playing in the sunlight beside our bows. Everywhere were little coral islands, some low and surrounded by shining beaches, some rising like domes from the water, and each clad luxuriantly in emerald foliage, still glistening from the moisture of a passing shower. Sea gulls lazily flapped their wings as they circled about us, and in the lagging breeze, native boats, with their brown hulls and ocher matting sails, slowly glided across the blue. Color was everywhere, and we knew that birds of brilliant plumage were swinging in the distant foliage, and schools of jeweled fishes flicking their rainbow fins among the coral.

"Isn't this a hell of a hole?" I recognized the speaker from the sentiment expressed, and turned to see the stocky captain who had been growling consistently all the way from San Francisco about losing two more years of his life.

"You see that island," he said, pointing toward Samar, "I spent six rotten months over there during the rainy season, picking leeches off of my legs and chasing *Pulajanes*, and I'll bet the scoundrel who killed the best sergeant I ever had is sitting up right now as *presidente* of some town and being patted on his fat belly and called `dear little brown brother' by some of the podunk politicians that are sent out here to keep us from governing these islands properly.

"What happened to your sergeant?" I inquired.

"The scoundrels," he growled, "they're a hell of a way from being little brown brothers of mine."

"He was about to pass on, when I detained him by pointing out a school of unusually large flying fish, sailing like dragon flies above the waves. His only comment was, "Yes, even the fish get tired of this damned Philippine water."

"But how did they happen to get your sergeant?" I asked, anxious to hear some of the experiences of a man whose operations in insurgent territory had succeeded where others had failed.

"Well," he said, "they weren't satisfied with having us splash around in the mud and get the dhobi itch up in Luzon, but sent my company down to a God-forsaken little barrio over here in Samar. I was the only officer with the company beside the captain, and we had a medico with us who had just come over from the States. By the time we'd been there a month, cholera broke out in the barrio, and the natives began to die off like flies. We boiled all of our water, ate nothing but cooked food out of boiled dishes, and kept the flies off of everything, so we got along very well, and only one soldier, who had eaten some fresh bananas from the market, doubled up and died.

"The natives used to collect in the big church every day and listen to the mestizo priest say prayers and ring the bell. The bell got to be a nuisance, and I wanted the captain to have it taken down, but he had some peculiar religious notions, and wouldn't do it.

"It was an awful job, getting the barrio cleaned up and the disease stopped, because the natives had so many superstitions that they wouldn't listen to common sense. They fired bamboo cannon to scare off the cholera spirit, they sang dirges, they put charms in front of their houses, but still they died. Every night they would set up a wailing in every house where anyone had died, and this, together with the dull boom of the bamboo cannon and the outlandish clanging of the church bell was enough to ruin anybody's rest.

"They died in their houses, they died in their banana patches, they died in the market place, and they died everywhere. They died faster than they could be buried, and sometimes everybody in one shack would pass out, and it wouldn't be found out for several days.

"We talked sanitation, we told them to clean up, our doctor worked with them day and night, but they wouldn't listen to us. We tried to get the mestizo padre to talk to them, but he never got beyond sprinkling them with holy water drawn from an infected well, and telling them the Americanos had brought the cholera.

"We turned out all the able-bodied *hombres* in town at the point of the bayonet and had a big burying. We found some that ought to have been buried a week before, all bloated and covered with flies that divided their time between the corpses and the market-place.

"Then we had a big clean-up. Burning all the refuse we could, we tried to keep the rest underground, but this was a hard job. We put sentinels over the wells to keep the fools away. Then we collected all the pots and kettles we could find, and allowed no one to get water until it had been boiled. After this, we made war on flies, and allowed nothing to be displayed in the market which was not covered up with some of their mosquito-bar cloth.

"The goo-goos didn't want to do a thing we told them, but we tightened up until they had to. Our non-commissioned officers worked themselves thin, inspecting, reporting cases, seeing that things were kept clean, and enforcing sanitary measures. Sergeant Dolan took it harder than anybody else, and acted as though a real calamity had happened every time a new hombre turned up his toes. He worked himself thin, and even went so far as to arrange for the parceling out of children, when their parents had died and nobody took the trouble to look after them.

"It wasn't long before we had the cholera by the neck, and when a week had passed without a case, the padre called a big meeting at the church and told his flock of black sheep that his prayers had been answered and that he had delivered them from the cholera, and announced that in a few days he had even greater blessings in store for them.

"Only three nights later, the little outpost which we had back of town was rushed and shot up by *insurrectos*. We all turned out and had an awful mix-up in the dark, but after several natives had been killed, the rest ran away. When we went to check up on our men, Sergeant Dolan, who had been in charge of the outpost that night, couldn't be found.

"I started out at dawn next morning with one platoon to try to roundup this bunch of insurrectos and get Dolan if he was still alive. I had a pretty good idea that the bunch came from the di-

14

rection of a little barrio at the base of the mountains about twelve miles off, so we made a bee line for that.

"When we were about a mile on our way, I heard the bell of the church we had just left ringing in a peculiar sort of way. It struck once, then there was a pause. Then came two taps, followed very shortly by three more. Another pause, and then six taps. The series was repeated twice. It started a third time but didn't finish. Someone must have stopped it. I began to try to figure out the meaning of the bell, when a corporal named Sanders came up and handed me a piece of paper which he had been writing on. What does the Lieutenant think of that?" he asked. I looked at the paper, and it bore these marks:

One = one officer
Two three = twenty-three men
Four = probably direction we are going
"You see, Sir," he added, "that's just how many we have."
"He had barely spoken when the same signal sounded half a mile in front of us, this time on a conch-shell horn or *budhan* as they call it.

"After we had arrived within about three miles of the barrio, we saw what appeared to be a man standing in the trail. When we got to it, we found it was Dolan's body, impaled on a bamboo stick with the feet dangling several inches from the ground. The top of his head had been cut off, the brains taken out and the cavity filled with mud, and as though this were not enough, he had been disemboweled and some of his entrails stuffed into his mouth.

"A fire was smoldering a few paces off the trail. One of the men noticed it, and walked over to look at a piece of paper which was lying near it. Just before he got there, the ground gave way under his feet, and he disappeared into a pitfall making a sickening noise. We pulled him out with a bamboo stake through each thigh, and a gash on his shoulder. After bandaging him up, our men made a litter out of two flannel shirts and a couple of poles to carry him on. Then we buried Dolan in the pit, and moved on toward the barrio.

"The trail led on through cogon grass about six feet high, and so thick you couldn't see a yard into it. It wasn't long before a volley of bullets came down the trail, killing two of the four men who were marching about a hundred yards up in front as a point. The rest of us spread out and tried to return the fire, but couldn't see much to shoot at. I sent one squad around to the right to outflank them, but had hardly gotten them started when the grass on our left began to swarm with bolo men, who rushed in among us and began to hack right and left. Luckily, we were marching with our bayonets fixed.

"There was pretty much of a mix-up for a few seconds, and then we let loose a little surprise party. We had four sawed-off Winchester pump guns loaded with buck shot, and when it comes to close-range work, nothing can touch one of these. The buck shot hadn't been flying long before there wasn't a native in sight, except about fifteen that weren't in shape to leave.

"I checked up on the men and found a couple with bad cuts, and then went back to look at the man on the litter. They had chopped him up. His left arm, which he had probably held up to protect his head, was cut off just above the wrist, and a gash across the face had finished him. The men who were carrying the litter said they had been engaged with half a dozen men on the left of the trail, when a brown arm with a bolo reached out from the grass on the other side of the trail and made the two slashes.

"When we got to the barrio, we found everything quiet and peaceful as a Sunday school meeting, and the head man had a cock -and-bull story about some *Pulajanes* who had just passed by on their retreat to the mountains. A bunch of men were working ex-tra hard repairing nipa thatch and doing other unnecessary things about the village. We rounded these up and had a search made for arms, but couldn't find as much as a pocket knife.

"Then we had some graves dug at the edge of a bamboo thick-et near the barrio, and led the natives out to a place within sight of them. I told one of the *hombres* that I wanted to know where those rifles were hidden, and that he had better be damned quick about telling me. All I could get out of him was, "*No sabe, Senor*," so I didn't waste any time having a couple of soldiers march him down and stand him up in front of one of the graves. He acted just as though he didn't think anything was going to happen to him. I told a corporal that I was ready. He lined up his firing squad, took careful aim, and fired. The *hombre* fell backwards into the grave.

"I called out another *hombre*, a measly looking old scoundrel with pockmarks all over his face. Where are the guns?' I said. The old fool immediately began to boo-hoo and hold his hands up toward the sky and swear he had never seen any guns, and to whimper a whole lot of twaddle about wanting to be the friend of the Americanos. When they had him half way down to the next grave, he looked as if he wanted to come back and talk, but the soldiers hurried him on, and when the firing squad cut loose, he dropped into his grave with a nice plunk.

"The next *hombre* I spoke to was the head man of the barrio, and he could hardly talk fast enough to tell us all he knew. Then he led us to a stack of straw not fifty yards away, and we found it was hollow and had sixteen rifles and a pile of bolos tucked away in it. When we had gotten the rifles, I yelled down in the direction of the graves, and the two *hombres* crawled out, along with the soldiers that had been hiding there and had yanked them in when the guns went off.

"We never had any more trouble in that district; but six months later I pretty nearly lost my commission trying to explain to some politicians in Manila why a certain native village went up in smoke. A hell of a thing to be called on to explain when one of the guns in that straw-stack was Dolan's."

When the Captain was gone, I looked up and saw the first of those exquisite sunsets which only he who visits tropical islands can feast his eyes upon. In our own country, we see a few colors in the western sky, a fiery ball drops behind the hilltops and a long twilight precedes the night. Not so in the tropics. Toward evening, great masses of white clouds begin to form and rise like huge columns into the sky. As the sun goes down, their dome-shaped crests climb higher and higher, catching and reflecting the light; and often while the upper part blazes like a pillar of fire, a shower floats down from the purple shadows at its base.

It was such a sunset that we saw in San Bernardino. Not only the west, but the entire sky began to blaze with colors unknown in temperate zones. The cloud-columns glowed with ever-changing reds - carmine, scarlet, ruby, wine-color, magenta and rose. Above these blazing masses, were little patches of mackerel, blowing like handfuls of coals thrown off into space and fanned into flame as they sped through the air. Higher still were filmy, thread-like streaks tinted with every hue, as though some master hand had swept his brush across the sky, leaving colors no mortal could name.

Above, the sky was still deep blue, shading almost imperceptibly through aquamarine into a clear vivid green. It is these shades of luminous green which are most distinctive in tropical sunsets. I have never seen them far from the equator, but have spent many a pleasant evening on the Luneta in Manila, watching them above Mariveles.

As the sun slowly drew toward the horizon, long rays of light shot out from it like the ribs of a fan, while a shower, coming from a wine-colored mass in the East, spanned a tiny coral island with a rainbow. Then the sun dropped behind the horizon. It was not twilight nor dusk; night came on at once.

CHAPTER III

Cebu - His Most Christian Majesty - The Siesta Hour - A Short Cut

When those intricate problems of how much to fee the bath steward, the room boy and the waiter had been solved, we gathered on deck in that garrulous state of excited activity which always marks the last day of a voyage. New frocks and freshly-starched khaki were in evidence, and from somewhere in the ship's depths there appeared those people who suddenly bob up at the end of a long journey and lead you to wonder when they got on.

The pale lettuce-green mountains of the Island of Cebú were over our bows. Like most of the mountains in the Philippines, their crests were sharp, and long knife-edged ridges, running down from the sky-line, gradually divided themselves into numerous narrow spurs. In the deep valleys between these spurs, we could see an impenetrable tangle of trees, vines and bamboo, while the ridges and summits stood out clearly, looking, from a distance as though covered by a well-clipped lawn.

The harbor of Cebú lies between the island of that name and the little island of Maktan. We soon rounded the end of Maktan, passed an old ruined watchtower and came into the harbor. On the low, palm-covered bench of land which skirts the island, lay the city of Cebú. The sun was beating down upon the red Spanish tiles of its roofs, and its pink and cream-colored stucco. The massive bell-towers of the churches wriggled and squirmed in the heated atmosphere, and the gray bastions of old fort San Pedro jutted out thirstily into the bay.

Four centuries before, the Spanish galleons of Magellan had sailed into this same harbor on their first voyage around the world. Like all who have followed him in trips to out-of-the-way places in tropical seas, one of Magellan's first acts was to write home about how he had hob-knobbed with native royalty. His records lead off with an account of how he was met on the beach by "the King" and two thousand warriors, of how he and this potentate formed an alliance by the "blood-compact," which consisted in exchanging drinks of each other's blood, and of many other exploits in which he and His Majesty were participants. His records even go so far as to mention "the princess." Had you ever picked up a book of travel among tropical islands which does not mention "the princess" in some such passage as this?: She stood by the sea, the shapely lines of her graceful figure accentuated by the simple garment rich was thrown so carelessly about her. There was sadness in those melting brown eyes, which should have gleamed with love and happiness. Perhaps she was thinking of the days when her people were free, and her ancestors were princes" - all this about a flat nosed native girl who looked rather ill at ease after too hearty a meal of lizards and grasshoppers.

But to return to Magellan. It appears that after a little conversation with the King, the latter, who had never before heard of Christianity or Spain, forthwith embraced the Christian religion and swore allegiance to the Spanish King.

Unfortunately, Magellan's association with royalty was far from resulting happily. Eager for excitement and anxious to show his royal ally that he would keep faith with him, he accompanied the King to Maktan on an expedition against a hostile tribe. It was here that an arrow from a naked savage ended the illustrious career of one of the world's boldest spirits and greatest navigators. Soon afterwards, Magellan's men were invited to a feast, where many died from the food which His Most Christian Majesty had poisoned. The few survivors then continued their journey around the world.

By noon, the troops which were to garrison Cebú, had exchanged places with those who were to return home, and we had waved a farewell to the remainder of our regiment, which sailed on to other ports. Four companies were soon settled in the old Spanish barracks, and the remaining two marched out to Guadalupe, about three miles inland at the foot of the hills. My own duties took me with the latter, and I was soon settled with several other officers in a little bamboo house overlooking the target range.

Scarcely had we thrown off our coats and stretched ourselves in our camp chairs, when we were besieged by a rabble of natives who sought to enlist their services as our "boys." They spoke in a mixed smattering of Spanish and English, and in various ways expressed their qualifications as servants.

"Me work long time *Teniente* Anderson, he *mucho* like *buen muchacho,"* said one, exhibiting a "recommendation" to the effect that he was lazy and a source of despair to anyone who might be so unfortunate as to employ him.

Next came a dapper-looking boy with an expression of decidedly snobbish superiority. "Sir, I was go to the school. I can do the student. I am servant of rare opportunity." This seemed to be the entire extent of his learning, for try as we would, we could get nothing more out of him but a repetition of his original speech.

One boy, who said that his name was Ambrosio Alizan, produced a bamboo joint containing seven recommendations. Well recommended, I thought, and began reading his papers. The first stated that Carlo Angeles Melino was an excellent horse boy. The second recommended Pedro Yacan as a cook. The third recommended Dolores Balanga for her faithful services as washerwoman. For fear that seven of these documents were insufficient, the boy explained that tomorrow he could get many more, but that today they were being used by his brother. Finally I selected a boy without literary appendages and with a peculiar stolid expression which in some way kept reminding me of an iguana. Having decided to employ him, I made inquiry concerning his domestic affairs.

"Got wife?" I asked. The imperturbable look never left his features.

"Some time got, some time no got," he replied.

Between getting ourselves and our troops settled, the day passed rapidly, and when night came, we found ourselves ready for bed. All but Whitson and I had gone to spend the night in Cebú, and within an hour after supper, we were carefully tucking in the mosquito bars around the edges of our bamboo cots.

There is something about the first night in a strange place that always sets the imagination adrift. Perhaps it is a faint recollection of the fairy tales of our childhood, that so often gives us fanciful thoughts; and as we lie half musing, half dreaming, fills our ears with vague whisperings, and leads us to picture weird shapes peering in at the window.

As I began to dose off, the almost human groaning of the bamboo, as its stems rubbed together in the gentle breeze, filled my drowsy mind with uncanny dreams. I could see long snaky arms with twisted fingers reaching out toward me, and cruel eyes gazing out of evil faces. As I dreamed all of this, a loud squawk, not two feet from my head, brought me to with a jolt. The squawk was followed by a deep, hoarse cry of "gek oh" which was repeated half a dozen times, gradually becoming fainter and ceasing as though from exhaustion.

I was sitting bolt upright in bed, blinking and wondering what on earth had happened, when I heard a subdued chuckle from the next cot. I turned toward Whitson. "What in the world is that thing?" I said. "Gecko," he replied.

I had already heard this remark from the creature itself, and therefore did not relish it from Bill. He soon explained further, however, that a gecko was nothing more than a harmless lizard about a foot long, gifted with a stentorian voice and sociable inclinations.

Next morning, after I had slid into my shoes, I noticed Whitson carefully pick up each of his, look into it, and shake it out. Upon inquiry, he informed me that during his last tour in the islands, he had stepped rather carelessly into one of his shoes, and that a centipede, who disputed its possession, had caused him to step out of it in a far less leisurely manner. Since then, part of his morning routine had always been to shake out his shoes.

Before another day had passed, the sky-line proved so inviting that I set out in the afternoon following a little trail which led toward the hilltops. I was scarcely a hundred yards from camp, when several large birds, which I took for pheasants, flew up with a whir and went sailing across a little valley.

I followed them with my eyes, and when they settled down near a bamboo shack a furlong away, was thoroughly surprised to find that they were nothing more than native chickens. These have a remarkable power of flight, due no doubt to their close kinship to the wild fowl of similar species which is found throughout the archipelago. You will rarely see a prouder bird than the Philippine wild cock. Early in the morning you can hear him crowing from the top of an anthill, and if you should chance to see him strutting beside his little brown mate, he cannot fail to win your admiration. In size, he is a trifle smaller than a game-cock, which in many respects he resembles. His head, adorned with a small comb, is carried high, and his black breast and tail make a striking contrast with the glistening red of his neck and body. His chief ornament is his tail, which though black, has a peculiar greenish sparkle when in the sun. It is longer and more luxuriant than that of a domestic cock, and when he flies, the two top feathers trail out a couple of feet behind him. Little wonder that a bird endowed with such plumage has learned to crow.

The path meandered about, among coconut palms and bamboo, past a number of native houses, each set up on stilts five or six feet from the ground. They were nearly all alike - a framework of bamboo, a steep roof thatched with the leaves of the nipa palm, and walls of the same material, held together by narrow strips of bamboo. Windows were cut in the walls, and each covered by a hinged flap of nipa. This could be propped up with a stick after the fashion of an awning, or allowed to hang down and cover the opening.

It was three o'clock in the afternoon, and no sign of human activity could be seen. It was the *siesta* hour, or to be accurate, one of the several hours devoted to the afternoon snooze. Through the open doorways, brown bodies could be seen sprawled out on the split bamboo floors. Pigs, chickens and goats, drowsy with the heat, blinked stupidly from beneath the houses; birds sat silently in the dense foliage, and everything appeared to be at a standstill. The only creatures that seemed condemned to activity were the cadaverous-looking dogs, which were eternally scratching at their mangy sides and biting frantically at the myriads of fleas which tormented them.

There are a few animals more disgusting, and withal more pathetic-looking than a native dog. His tail is always between his legs and he has the hunted look of a creature without hope. The remnant of hair that the mange has left on his back, is usually short and nondescript in color. He is rarely fed, and then only with the most disgusting offal; and in his half-starved condition, his bones almost protrude through the skin. He never follows his master abroad, but throughout the day lies in the dirt under the house, and emerges after dark to make night hideous by his unearthly howling, barking, snarling and yelping. But despise him as we may, we cannot forget that he still puts faith in the humans who maltreat him, and that he looks up and wags his tail when his master returns home, and licks the hand that puts food out of his reach and then beats him for sucking eggs.

Before long, the trail started up one of the spur-like foothills, following its crest to the top of the main ridge. West of this, the mountains rose in waves of ever-increasing height, until the sky-line marked the back-bone of the island. To the eastward the hills of Bohol broke the horizon, and Maktan stretched itself like a barrier in front of the long, narrow harbor. A plain, dotted with palms and mango trees, lay between the foothills and the sea. Scattered about on this plain were groups of native shacks, and as the cool of the evening approached, little columns of blue smoke began to rise from among them. On the thread-like paths, brightly-colored specks could be seen moving about. The *siesta* was over, and the activities of the evening had commenced.

I sat absorbed in the scene below me until nearly sundown, and then started home. I had come by a round-about way, but as I could see camp directly below, I decided to save time by taking the shortest route. The way looked clear, so I started out at a brisk gait, with visions of a good supper ahead of me.

The grass, which was waist-high on the ridge, soon became breast-high, shoulder-high, and then well above my head. With increasing difficulty, I pushed my way through it as I descended. Soon I became sensible of numerous little cuts on my hands and face, caused by the sharp edges of thin grass, but as camp seemed so very near, I was tempted to push on. Finally, I became exhausted and sat down. It was sundown when I left the ridge, and it was suddenly brought home to me that the twilight was only a matter of a few minutes, and night had come. I could go no further through the "lawn" which I had seen from below, so groped my way back to the trail, and returned the way I had come.

I reached camp, tired and hungry, and found Bill Whitson sitting in his camp-chair enjoying an after-dinner cigar. Bill had spent several years in the Philippines, and had learned the art of making himself comfortable. He looked with decided amusement at my cut hands and generally frazzled condition.

"Get lost?" he said. "No, short cut," I replied. He smiled, and turned to one of our newly-acquired servants. "Boy, fix bath; get chow; fix bed." I acquiesced.

CHAPTER IV
Inebriate Aviation - Pink Goats - Racing Corpses

Early one morning I was passing through a coconut grove near my house and happened to look up at one of the bamboo joints in which the natives catch their tuba. The sun had barely risen, and the fermenting liquid had not yet been gathered. As I glanced up, my eye was caught by a bedraggled, dilapidated looking bird, with feathers all awry, hopping laboriously from frond to frond toward the bubbling vessel of tuba.

He had every appearance of being an old soak, and in fact, he was. He perched himself on the edge of the bamboo joint, stuck his beak into its contents, and had his morning nip. Evidently, it did him good, for he hopped to a leaf-stem just above, shook his feathers into more presentable shape, cocked his head on one side and surveyed the world with an air of decided satisfaction.

After he had preened himself for a while, the idea struck him that it was time for another drink. In fact, the idea recurred to him very frequently, and after each libation, his tail rose a notch higher and his entire being seemed to expand with the glories of his existence. He began to sing, and put his whole soul into it, trilling notes an octave higher than anything we had ever heard before.

The shaded seclusion of a palm was no fitting place for so rare and gifted a bird. With his head cocked more than ever, he dimly saw a leafless *dol-dol* tree, with a tall switch sticking up from its top. It was the highest and most conspicuous place in sight, and he made for it.

He took deliberate aim, but to his great surprise he missed his chosen perch by a foot. With some difficulty, he swung round in a large circle, and tried again. On the third attempt, he slowed up, and with a desperate grab, caught the switch in his toes as he went by.

The switch being vertical he could not perch on it, but clung for a moment in an awkward posture, afraid to let go. Finally, completely mystified by the tree's behavior, he fluttered down into a thicket to sleep off his jag. Doubtless you can still find him, taking his daily eye-opener and filling the air with his song, unless dissipation has cut short his happy existence and sent him to a drunkard's grave.

Part of my work took me to Cebú every day, a three-mile ride along a road lined with native houses. In front of every shack, tied by the leg to a small peg in the ground, was the most important member of the family, the game-cock. Each cock was attached in such a way as almost, but not quite, to permit him to reach his next-door neighbor; and was thus kept in a perpetual state of ruffling up his feathers, straining at his string, scowling gallinaceous profanity at his rival, and then crowing himself hoarse.

A large part of a Filipino's morning is occupied in the training and exercising of his cock. The normal procedure usually includes a bath and rubdown, and, strange to say, the bird appears to relish both.

A chicken's preparations for the pit are certainly made at the expense of his appearance. He is usually pruned of his comb and wattles, his tail shortened, and most of the feathers of his neck and back removed. This allows the sun to shine on his bare skin, which soon acquires the bright red color of the flesh on his head.

There appears to be a strong bond of friendship between one of these game-cocks and his master. A native will scarcely ever pet a dog, but I have seen him squat for hours stroking and fondling his rooster, while the latter chuckled and gurgled his appreciation. Often, after being petted, one of these roosters will sidle up to his master, hopping on one leg, and kicking out with the opposite foot and wing, exactly as our own barnyard fowl makes flirtatious advances toward a dignified old hen.

During the week, he absorbs the greater part of his master's time and attention. On Sunday, he goes to the *bulangan* to win a pocket-full of silver pesos, or be cut down by the stroke of a gaff and thrown into a corner to die.

About the second morning that I rode in, I encountered, in the middle of the road, a pink goat with green horns. I reined in my horse, rubbed my eyes, and wondered if I was in my right mind. "No, there ain't no such animal," I reflected. When the horse pricked up his ears, I realized that he saw it too, and felt better.

Further on, I passed a green duck and a lavender puppy. When I reached town, I had considerable hesitancy in telling anyone what I had seen. Eventually, I learned that the Visayan has a great fondness for coloring any animal which nature intended to be white. The possibilities of this particular form of art are amazing.

Among the happy characteristics possessed by the Filipino is his ability to take the death of a friend or near relative very lightly. This, coupled with his desire to find in everything the excuse for a celebration, makes a funeral one of the most delightful of his social diversions.

It is only among the wealthy, however, that the corpse can enjoy the luxury of riding to his final resting place in the ornate hearse, which Cebú regards as a masterpiece in funereal art. This vehicle has glass sides, through which the bright colors of the coffin may be seen surrounded by a shiny railing. The woodwork of the hearse is painted white, and covered with elaborate carvings in the shape of beads, wreaths and draperies. On the four upper corners, are sockets into which are fitted large feather-dusters, their color depending upon the general color-scheme of the funeral. Very often, it is pink, in which case, there are usually large stripes of this color painted on the coffin, and pink plumes stuck into the head-pieces of the bridles between the horses' ears.

Scarcely of less prominence than the corpse himself, is the driver. Somewhere, perhaps from the left-overs of a fancy-dress ball, he has acquired the cocked hat and blue-and-buff uniform of one of our "minute men" of 1776.

Beside the hearse march brightly attired pallbearers, their number and costumes depending somewhat upon the opulence of the deceased. Leading the procession is a band, playing all the catchy comic opera airs which it has picked up by ear. In rear of the hearse are strung out the mourners, often well primed with their native drink of tuba, and wearing an expression of intense satisfaction.

But it is only the wealthy *gente fino* that can be buried in such style. The ordinary *tao* must content himself with much less pomp. As a matter of pride, he likes to ride to the cemetery in a coffin, preferably a pink-and-green striped one with a skull and cross-bones painted on one end and R.I.P. on the other. Since it is a shame, both from the standpoint of art and of economy to bury so handsome a container, the coffin can be rented for the funeral, and returned when the corpse, carefully tied up in matting, has been dumped to rest.

A hearse being financially out of reach, transportation is furnished by four stalwart natives, who swing the coffin on a couple of bamboo poles and carry it on their shoulders. The way is too long and the sun too hot to make the trip without a stop; and when the bearers stop from time to time under the shade of a tree by the roadside, the coffin furnishes a convenient seat, while they rest and smoke a cigarette. Music in some form usually accompanies the procession, and the mourners follow on foot, often carrying some such delicacy as a roast pig, which is eaten with great relish after the ceremony.

The cemetery lies half-way between Cebú and Guadalupe, and on my daily rides, I most frequently encountered these funerals. One morning, as I was overtaking a particularly inebriate-looking procession, another of similar character cut in from a side road and attempted to get ahead of it. Not wishing their charge to be passed on his heavenward journey, the bearers on the main road slightly increased their pace. Not to be outdone, those turning in from the side road did likewise, and swung in abreast of them. Both then broke into a trot, and the race was on.

The mourners for Pedro cheered lustily for their corpse; while the bereft followers of his rival shouted encouragement to the remains of Juan. It was the pink coffin of Juan that first took the lead, but in the final spurt, it was the green one that led the way through the cemetery gate; and the name of Pedro was registered first upon the list of heavenly arrivals.

CHAPTER V

A Spanish House - "Epidermis" and the Ill-Advised Exchange –The Killing of Narciso and Martin - The Deadly Greased Plate -Fishing in the Dust

It was not many weeks before I changed my abode from Guadalupe to Cebú. There were five bachelors in the garrison, and being gregarious by nature, we arranged to live under one roof. The house had formerly been the residence of a well-to-do Spaniard, and was characteristic of its type. There was a massive medieval look about the gray walls of its foundations, and its ponderous roof of red tiles, partly overgrown with moss and sprouting grass and ferns at the eaves. Altogether, it gave the appearance of having been cunningly devised by a mind which was keen at providing luxuries, but sufficiently thoughtless to overlook a number of necessities.

The first floor was of stone, with an arched driveway passing through it to the walled garden in rear. Beyond a well, a storehouse and facilities for keeping several horses and a couple of vehicles, there was nothing else on this floor, the living quarters being higher where they could catch the cool breezes and be away from the dust of the street.

A broad stairway of blue-and-white porcelain tiles led from the driveway to a spacious hall on the second floor. This adjoined the dining room and *sala,* the doorways being sufficiently broad and numerous to throw the whole into one large ballroom on occasions of festivity. The floors were of beautifully-polished hardwood, the planks being a foot wide and alternately light and dark. We kept these polished by having our boys tie burlap around their feet and dance around the room. The one whose dance was least entertaining we required to dance half an hour longer than the rest. This always made the floor-polishing a highly diverting spectacle of competitive pivoting, pirouetting and wild waving of arms.

Overlooking the garden, was a tile *azotea* with a stone railing, where many an old Spaniard had sat among his orchids and airplants, enjoying a smoke and a bottle of Madeira in the cool of the evening.

The second story was of wood and projected several feet beyond the first, thus providing room for two outer walls with a passageway between them. The window-panes were made of translucent shells, and the windows slid into recesses like folding doors, opening up almost the whole side of the house at once. Every window was shaded from above by a *midia-agua* of split bamboo and the large space between the ceiling and roof kept a free circulation of air overhead. The tropical sun has little effect upon such a house.

The kitchen was manifestly an afterthought, and was stuck onto the rear corner of the house like a martin-box and supported from the ground by two heavy wooden posts. The white ants eventually ate up everything but the outer shells of these posts, and we awoke one night to find that the rear half of the kitchen had dropped off.

As for the bathroom, it was non-existent. Behind a bamboo screen on one end of the *azotea* we found a large earthenware water-jar and a dipper. This primitive shower-bath had hitherto satisfied every want of our predecessors. We improved upon it by mounting a water-barrel on a tripod, putting a spigot in the bottom of the barrel and attaching the spout of a watering-pot to the mouth of the spigot. With plenty of boys to keep the barrel filled, we found this a very satisfactory arrangement.

Beside the cook and seven boys to look after our personal wants, we had a washerwoman named Epifania. If permitted to do so, the average Filipino *lavendera* will take your clothes to a social gathering of her kind around a dirty puddle, lay them on a rock, and pound them with a paddle until the buttons are all cracked. She will then return them looking beautifully white, but smelling vilely and full of germs.

To prevent this, we required Epifania, or "Epidermis," as we always called her, to do her work under the house. This took her pretty much all week, and at almost any hour of the day, she could be seen sitting on the coping of the well, her flat face puckered around a huge, black cigar, and her bare brim arms busily rubbing the clothing, or pushing the hollow flat-iron with a charcoal fire burning inside of it, and a chimney at its front end.

Epifania had two possessions. One was a cadaverous-looking goat, which she kept tethered on the best part of the lawn; the other was a fat husband, who either slept under a banana tree in the garden, or squatted near the goat and smoked cigarettes. Whenever the succulent grass of our lawn began to fatten the goat into convex curves resembling those of the husband, Epifania would straightaway dispose of the former animal and appear next morning with another skeleton. On Sunday, Epifania would array herself in a bright red skirt, a fresh yellow *panuelo* and a green umbrella, and go to church. The husband, meanwhile, would spend the day, and most of Epifania's money at the cock-fight. What we could never understand was why, of her two possessions, it was the goat which she always exchanged.

Shortly after we had become established, we were sitting at lunch and heard a violent commotion in the kitchen. Angry voices were raised to a high pitch, and Visayan epithets were flying loose. I walked out to the kitchen and stopped in the doorway. In the middle of the floor, my own boy, Narciso, and Tucker's boy, Martin, were standing six inches apart, yelling angrily at the top of their voices. Narciso was brandishing a butcher knife, which he appeared to be about to plunge into Martin's heart, while the latter seemed ready to split Narciso's head with a cleaver. Ramon, the cook, was at the stove, completely absorbed in frying some red bananas.

"Narciso," I said, "would you like to kill Martin?

"Yizzir," he answered, and tried to explain why, but I stopped him.

"Martin, would you like to kill Narciso?"

"Me kill him," was the morose reply. "Too much *habla*, not enough kill." I announced, "Cornelio, get mop and bucket." The latter produced these implements. I pointed to the clock; it was seventeen minutes of one.

"Quarter of one, you begin fight. Ten minutes of one, if Narciso dead, Martin clean up blood on floor. If Martin dead, Narciso clean up blood of Martin."

With this remark, I returned to the dining room. Considerably more than one minute before quarter of one, I heard the tinkle of two weapons upon the kitchen floor, and the sound of bare feet moving rapidly in divergent directions. Thereafter there was peace in the kitchen.

However, the restoration of peace did not reduce the amount of conversation. A *muchacho* who is not kept busy, is inclined to become garrulous and lazy; so when we found that our boys had sufficient leisure time to squat around the kitchen and chatter like so many monkeys, we had to invent some new form of occupation to keep them hopping. This was not as easy as it might seem, for eight boys can arrange, fold, wipe, dust, clean and polish about everything in one house in a remarkably expeditious manner.

It was a Chinaman who finally supplied the idea. I was in his little shop one hot afternoon getting some chocolate beans for our morning beverage, and his small boy was waiting on me. The old *Chino* was sitting in a dark corner about half asleep, but evidently much annoyed by half a dozen mosquitoes which kept buzzing around his ears. After making several vigorous but ineffectual slaps at his tormentors, he walked into the next room, and returned straightaway to his seat carrying a tin plate greased with lard. The mosquitoes renewed their attack, but this time to their own destruction. Whenever one of these luckless creatures buzzed within range, the long, yellow arm would reach out and slap him with the tin plate. His legs and wings would at once stick to the grease, and after a couple of kicks, he would be dead. Within five minutes, the plate, with half a dozen little black spots on it, was dropped on the floor, and the leathery features of the Chinaman relaxed into an expression of drowsy contentment. I turned to the boy. "Give me five tin plates," I said.

The mosquitoes which destroy our good temper in the evening, are nearly always to be found during the day sleeping off their night's orgy in the dark corners of the house. They roost behind pictures on the wall, in closets, under beds, in shoes, behind draperies and in the folds of unused clothing. When routed out of such places by the energetic use of a feather-duster, they fly slowly and groggily about the room, making superb targets for the anointed tin plate. At last, we had it: The boys were to spend their leisure time hunting mosquitoes; there would be no more chattering in the kitchen to disturb us by day, and no more buzzing about our ears to injure our amiability in the evening.

The scheme worked beautifully - at least, it worked beautifully with all but Narciso, and eventually it did with him. Somewhere in the recesses of Narciso's skull he had an object called an intellect, and this, after great effort, he occasionally managed to use. This was one of the occasions. To begin with, leisure was one of his hobbies, and this was seriously interfered with by the quest of the nimble mosquito. Something, therefore, must be done to end this leisure-destroying occupation.

One day, while I was sitting in my room reading, Narciso entered, as usual, with his feather duster, and tin plate. Something in the way he looked at me attracted my attention sufficiently for me to notice that the plate, instead of being lightly greased with lard, was streaming with something resembling olive oil. A mosquito was soon flushed, and after a vigorous flourish on the part of my boy, a long row of oily dots appeared on the wall. Another flourish, and another row of dots. When all of the oil had been transferred from the plate to the walls and ceiling, Narciso departed with a look of great satisfaction.

A few minutes later, I handed him a piece of paper upon which was written "1 bottle of household ammonia." "Narciso," I said, "Signe to the *botica*, give paper, get bottle, bring back *-pronto*."

The next two days he spent in removing grease-spots from the wall, after which he became the most expert of all our mosquito hunters.

Our house was on the main plaza of the town, near where it was joined by the principal street, *calle* Magallanes. An old Spanish church was on one side, and opposite this, the barracks. A path, running diagonally across the plaza, was the main thoroughfare to the market, and across this, the natives streamed from the earliest hours of the morning. Nearly all were well laden with articles which they were taking to offer for sale at the market, or less valuable commodities which they had bought and were taking home.

Little regard was paid to the comfort of any animal which might be so unfortunate as to make this journey to market. Chickens were usually tied together in bunches by the legs and carried, head downward on the end of a stick. Pigs usually had holes cut in their ears, and were dragged along, squealing, by a rope passed through the holes. If the pig proved obdurate, he usually had his feet tied together, a bamboo pole passed between his legs, and this carried between the shoulders of two natives.

Most of the carrying was done by women, and nearly all of

their burdens were borne on their heads. Anything from an egg or a bottle up to a barrel can be found balanced on the heads of these native women. From the time they can toddle about, whatever they wish to carry is transported in this way, and by the time they are grown, their heads become decidedly useful. A favorite form of torch for a woman moving about at night is a bottle filled with oil, with a lighted wick protruding from the neck. The bottle is placed upright on top of her head, and I have yet to see one drop off.

It is perhaps this habit of balancing articles on her head that gives the average native woman the superbly-erect rounded neck, and beautifully carried shoulders that are to be envied by any race. Perhaps from the same cause, however, she has acquired a shambling gait, totally devoid of springiness, keeping her feet close to the ground, and swinging her arms diagonally behind her. This swinging of the arms is a noticeable racial characteristic, as is the decidedly wide angle at which the feet are turned outward while walking. In this latter characteristic, the Filipino differs widely from the American Indian, who is inclined to turn his feet inward and walk in a slightly pigeon-toed fashion.

In matter of dress, the costumes of the women differ only in color, texture and ornamentation, but never in style or cut. For the Visayan woman, there are no such problems as: Where will the waist line be next season? Are they wearing them full or narrow? Following some medieval Spanish custom, the skirt is made with a train, but since this would drag on the ground, she habitually picks it up and tucks it away under her belt. Her *camisa* or waist, is low-necked and transparent, with broad sleeves reaching to the elbow, and is made of some material resembling stiffly-starched mosquito bar covering a white sleeveless *camiseta*. Another piece of stiff mosquito bar is folded into a triangle, placed around her shoulders and the ends crossed and pinned or tied over her breast. Her legs are bare, and her feet usually thrust into *chinelas*. These are leather sandals without heels, but with tips of green or red cloth into which she slides her toes. How these are kept on, is a matter of mystery to the white man, but she has no difficulty in going up and down stairs, or even dancing in them. Her long, straight hair is pulled back tightly enough to preclude the presence of any wrinkles in her forehead, and secured in a knot at the back of her head.

Always she wears vivid colors, her skirt being usually bright yellow, red, green or orange, and her *camisa* and *panuelo* [blouse and handkerchief]of a paler tint. Her clothing is always neat, and well-kept. As we go farther from town, we find her wearing less, sometimes with only the skirt, in which case the belt is fastened just under her arms, and passes above her breasts.

As for the man, he wears a hat, usually of straw, a colored shirt, and a pair of white trousers or drawers. The tail of the shirt, either as a matter of ornament or comfort, is left out. If the weather is particularly hot, the shirt tail is often rolled up under the arms, thus leaving a broad, brown expanse to be fanned by the cooling breeze.

The smaller children wear nothing. At the age of six or seven, they usually fall heir to some sort of a shirt, which is invariably one inch too short, at ten or eleven, they graduate into the regalia of their parents.

Of these children, there were always a number playing in the plaza. Their enjoyment was never expressed by the yells, screams, and wild outbursts of laughter with which Caucasian children give vent to their exuberance of spirits, but in their own way, they seemed to be having a thoroughly good time. They all enjoyed baseball, and played it from the time they were old enough to toss a betel nut and bat it with a stick.

The gambling instinct rises early in the Filipino, just as it does in our own race; and while our children are playing marbles and spiking tops "for keeps," the natives of the Philippines are staking their pennies on some game of their own invention. As surely as two native boys come together, each having a [copper] "clacker," no time is lost until some game is started whereby one of the boys becomes possessor of both "clackers." Most of these games are some modification of our own game of pitching a penny at a crack; but as the "clackers" are usually few, the game is correspondingly complicated, in order to prolong the excitement.

Often I had seen children on the plaza engaged in what appeared to be a terrestrial form of trout fishing. Each child was armed with a slender bamboo pole, to the end of which was attached a single strand of hemp several feet long, having a tiny noose in the end of it. To satisfy my curiosity one day, I turned my field glasses on a boy, wearing a pink-and-white striped cheesecloth shirt, who was deeply absorbed in this form of sport. He caught sight of something in the grass, and pole in hand, began stalking it after the fashion of a cat sneaking up on a young bird. Upon arriving sufficiently near, he slowly lowered the noose. A moment later, he gave the pole an upward jerk, while a large green object fluttered and kicked on the end of his line. After removing the legs and wings from this object, he proceeded to eat it with great relish. It was a huge grasshopper, nearly four inches long.

He continued his angling for some time, but the remainder of his catch he strung on a long bamboo splinter, evidently with a view to taking it home and cooking it for supper. Grasshoppers or locusts, properly cooked, are reputed to be decidedly shrimp-like in taste. In order to enjoy this delicate flavor, I have from time to time eaten shrimp.

Just why the world's greatest riders are not Filipinos, I have never been able to understand, for their training in this respect starts with infancy. As soon as a baby is old enough to be carried about, which is anywhere from a few hours to a few days, his mother puts him astride of her hip, and with one arm supporting his back, starts about her daily affairs. After several months, the child has developed sufficient strength in its legs to render the mother's assistance almost unnecessary. Perhaps the young monkey, which clings to its mother as she leaps from branch to branch, is not so many generations away, after all.

As a matter of fact, Darwin could have spent some very satisfactory days in the Philippines. The prehensile toe would have been his greatest source of delight. He could have seen natives from the mountains with their great toes set almost at right angles to the others; bull-cart drivers holding their reins with their toes; children perched in the upper branches of trees using their toes, instead of their hands, to hold on with; and women with baskets on their heads, picking up articles from the ground with these prehensile members. Shoes are a great handicap to the average Filipino.

Except during the siesta hours, there was never a time when the plaza was not full of life and movement. Chinamen in blue pajamas shuffled by, each carrying a pole on his shoulder with a heavy earthenware jar suspended from each end. Brown-armed women in red and yellow calico, swung by with baskets of fruit on their heads, or paused to gossip with their friends. A big bull carabao, with a boy perched on his back, ruminated sleepily in the shade of a tree. Pigs, tied up in banana-stalk slats, and balanced on the heads of women, squealed violent protest as they moved toward the market. Carabao carts, with solid wooden wheels, rumbled along under heavy loads of copra and hemp. Itinerant lace and embroidery vendors wandered about seeking the house of an Americano. Beggars made their weekly trip to the church, where the padre gave each a large, copper clacker.

Everywhere there was a profusion of colored umbrellas. Their fondness for these, seems not to arise from a fear of rain nor a dislike for the sun, but as an ornamental plaything, the umbrella has brought delight to the Filipino for many generations. Both men and women are happy under its shadow, and have been so for centuries. Years before the advent of the Spaniards, an old Chinese navigator, writing of the Philippines, stated that when it was desired to trade with the people of these islands, it was first very important to present umbrellas to their "mandarins," after which everything was easy.

Think of being able to keep the same fad for so many centuries, instead of having to wrack their brains for a new one every season!

CHAPTER VI

The Departed Spirit - Damask and Lizards - The Indigestion Party – Ramon

One of the least irritating methods of being roused from slumber is to be waked by your Filipino boy. In the course of your dreams you are vaguely conscious of an almost inaudible grunt. You sleep on, and in a few moments, a second little grunt has just enough effect on you to make you feel as though you had been half awake, and were dozing off again very pleasantly. A third grunt, slightly louder, leads you to stretch yourself and enjoy the feeling that you have had an altogether satisfactory rest.

As the grunts become louder, it gradually begins to dawn upon you that they are emanating from an object dressed in white, which is standing near your bed. For a while you wonder who it is, and then slowly recognize your boy. By the time you have raised yourself on one elbow, you think that you must have sent for him; for there he is with the very things you want: your bath robe, slippers, and a towel. In a few moments, an invigorating, cool shower-bath puts you on your toes. It is a delightful way to end your siesta.

Next to being waked himself, there are few things that a Filipino objects to more than waking someone else. There is a common superstition that when a man sleeps, his spirit takes a trip to some faraway land of dreams. If you wake him suddenly, he is liable to do some terrible thing before his soul has had time to get back to him. When you return to your *calesa* and shake the sleeping driver whom you always find curled up on the seat, a glance at his blear-eyed, vacant expression is almost enough to convince you that there is considerable truth in this belief.

One evening I returned from my shower to find that instead of the usual white uniform and change of clothing, Narciso had laid out my mess jacket and put studs into a stiff-bosomed, shirt. It occurred to me that I had overlooked telling him to prepare these, and had not even mentioned the fact that I was going out to dinner that night.

"Narciso," l said, "what for you fix mess jacket?" "Sir," he replied, "it iss dinner of the *Comandante.*" By some strange underground channel of information, our boy nearly always managed to keep track of our engagements. More than once, I have been reminded of some dinner by finding my dinner clothes laid out, without my having said a word to Narciso about it.

We had fallen into the Spanish custom of taking a drive in the cool of the evening and dropping in on one or two friends before dark; and ordering a *calesa*, I picked up another bachelor, and started out to make a few calls. At each house, we sat on the broad, screened porch, sheltered with vines and hung with air plants, and were offered tea, a tinkling glass of iced lemonade, or a little Scotch and soda. We talked of our last stations and conjectured at our next, we planned trips to China, to India and Japan, we discussed the problems and riddles of the East - and perhaps we gossiped a little. Being bachelors, we could not fail to touch upon feminine frivolities, or express views upon how to keep wives from gaining the upper hand, and the proper way to bring up children. Altogether, the time passed rapidly and pleasantly.

By seven-thirty, a dozen of us were on the Colonel's *azotea*, sitting in commodious chairs of wicker, or carved wood and rattan. They were built for the tropics, these chairs, large, cool and comfortable; and their broad arms, extending several feet beyond the seat, provided a convenient leg-rest while smoking a pipe or enjoying a good book.

When the guests had all arrived, two boys appeared. Each bore a tray of polished hardwood, the bottom of which was lined with plate glass, covering the embroidered likeness of a Peacock and golden pheasant. On one tray, was a plate of Russian caviar on toast and a pile of tiny napkins; on the other, a tinkling silver cocktail-shaker and a dozen glasses.

When our appetites had been whetted by "heel-taps" from the beaded cock-tail shaker, the boy announced, "Deenair eas sairb, mom," and we entered the dining room. Huge air plants hung in the broad windows, and a dozen orchids were blooming in swinging baskets made from the fibrous husks of coconuts. The table was decorated with fern leaves and the delicate coral-pink flowers of the *cadena de amor* Embroidered napkins showed the careful, painstaking work of Filipino needlewomen, and the damask cloth was of the shining whiteness which characterizes those obtainable in the Orient.

Tiny paper baskets at each place, held toasted pili nuts. No one has ever gotten enough pili nuts. Perhaps the only reason why they have not taken the place of salted almonds elsewhere is that no one without the patience of an oriental can ever be induced to crack a sufficient quantity of the iron-like shells for a meal. They have a most delicate flavor, and although crisp, are almost tender enough to be crushed with the tongue. If lighted, one of them will burn like a candle, a fact which was commentated upon and demonstrated at every dinner which I attended during my first year at Cebú.

Bouillon was served in little covered cups of Royal Medallion Canton ware. Then came prawns from the bay, and snipe on toast showed that the Colonel had a successful hunt in the rice fields.

The boys moved noiselessly about on their bare feet, here and there replenishing a basket with pili nuts, or filling a glass with sauterne. A salad of papayas and pomelos was brought in, followed by mango ice. Then came coffee.

Throughout the dinner, we could hear the cheerful cricket-like chirping of the house lizards which come out in the evening to catch mosquitoes and other insects. They are frail little things, their tails being particularly brittle; but in case of an accident to this member, they seem to have no difficulty in growing a new one.

Several of these lizards were on the ceiling above the table, where they had gathered to catch such millers and other insects as were attracted by the light. One of them, a very small one, was cautiously stalking a large moth, nearly as big as he was. Very stealthily he approached, inch by inch, just as a cat might sneak across the lawn toward a sparrow which was engrossed in swallowing a worm. When about three inches from his prey, the lizard gave a sudden rush and seized the moth in his jaws. But he had fastened on to more than he had bargained for. His sudden rush had loosened his hold on the ceiling, and the first violent flutter of the moth's large wings sent him tumbling toward the table.

Down he came, wriggling and squirming, and landed squarely in a cup of coffee. There was a moment of violent spluttering, and then a little streak shot across the white table cloth and onto the floor, leaving tiny brown footprints. Not even did it pause to look back at the dismembered tail, which had struck the rim of the cup, and was giving a few convulsive farewell waves from the edge of the saucer.

We chatted for a while after dinner, and, as the next day was to be Sunday, planned the route of our weekly morning ride. A group of us, about twenty in number, were in the habit of starting at sunrise every Sunday morning and riding for a couple of hours along the seashore or into the hills. Thoughts of the early start next day took us home a trifle earlier than usual, and by eleven-thirty we were all tucked away under our mosquito bars.

Early next morning, I heard the lusty voice of Pat Rafferty, the Collector of Customs, under my window. In addition to customs, he had collected some two hundred pounds of embonpoint, all of which he saddled upon a tiny Filipino pony which looked smaller than he. Rafferty, or "The Colonel," as we usually called him, never failed to show up for a ride, always mounted on his little, iron-gray stallion. When we started out, no one ever expected the little animal to get back alive. As Rafferty swung his weight into the saddle, the pony's head and tail would fly up with a jerk, his back sway downward, and the skin on his belly grow perceptibly tighter. Some humanitarian member of the party even suggested that the Colonel wear roller skates, in order to ease the strain on his horse. But the strength and toughness of these ponies is remarkable, and the end of the ride always found this little fellow fresh and in the best of spirits, usually nibbling at his master's pockets for a lump of sugar.

By the time the boys had brought our horses around, several officers, some ladies, a couple of Englishmen, and some other civilians had collected in the plaza, and we were ready to start.

We trotted off in pairs, and as we reached the edge of town, were joined by a Mrs. Wyslezemus and her daughter. With such a name, it is not surprising that she was universally known as Mrs. Whistling Jesus. Her husband, the Judge, did not show up, but had arranged to spend the morning with a Jap who was giving him lessons in ju-jitsu. This form of sport had recently become his hobby, and he took great delight in demonstrating his newly-acquired holds at the club. Here he would approach some peaceful and unsuspecting victim, stick one thumb into his eye and the other into a tender spot beneath his ear, and then enthusiastically show that great suffering could be produced by placing his heel against the shin bone or his knee against the small of the back.

As our horses reached the rolling foothills at Mabolo, the sun was just bursting from a golden mass of clouds beyond Maktan. The air was invigorating, and everything full of life. Women were gathering mangos from the dark green sphere-shaped trees upon which they grew, or moving toward town with baskets of fruit and other edibles on their heads. All the men whom we passed had roosters under their arms and were bound for the *bulangan* where they drank *tuba*, gambled and fought cocks until dark.

Flocks of green-backed doves with yellow along their flanks were feeding in the open fields, and flew up as we passed. Rain crows were gurgling with their peculiar jug-like note, and kites were sailing about, looking for their breakfast. I saw one of them pounce down, rise with a large snake in his talons, and go flapping off toward the mountains.

At length we turned toward the beach and reached it near Mandaue, at a point where the natives were getting salt from the ocean. They had a number of shallow basins into which they pumped sea water by means of crude wheels and tread-mills. When partly evaporated, the water was then let into still shallower basins, and when the sun had completely dried these up, the salt was scraped from the bottom, and collected into sacks woven from palm leaves. These salt factories always went out of business during the rainy season.

It was eight-thirty when we pulled up in front of Dr. Pond's and turned our horses over to the boys. Pond had at one time been a professional baseball pitcher, but had taken to medicine and established himself in Cebú. It soon became his function to look after the health of the island, and due to his untiring efforts, he had practically wiped out the cholera, and was now devoting himself to a war against leprosy and other prevalent diseases.

Mrs. Pond had about six dogs, who greeted us loudly as we approached. She spoke to them in Spanish. One of them, a venerable-looking dog of non-descript breed, seemed to be her favorite. He appeared to understand everything she told him. His large eyes were always fixed admiringly upon her, and he cocked his ears and wagged his tail whenever she spoke. He was a very old dog, grizzled about the muzzle, and walked with the laborious, stiff-legged gait which showed that the brief span of years which nature had allowed him was nearly at an end.

Mrs. Pond had been planning for some time to return and spend a year in the States, but the United States laws do not permit dogs to be imported from the Philippines. She knew that if she left old Fritz he would die of grief during her absence, and had therefore decided not to leave Cebú during the one or two years which the faithful old dog still had ahead of him.

As a change from the conventional meals to which we were accustomed, our hostess had decided to serve this one in Filipino fashion. Accordingly, we were all seated on mats on the broad, hardwood verandah, and a delicious breakfast served with banana leaves as plates and coconut shells to drink from. As a preliminary, however, we had some sort of an eye-opener in a tall glass, which banished all thoughts of being tired, and acted as a decided stimulus to conversation.

When breakfast was over, and we had talked a while, the boys saddled our horses, and we returned home individually.

It was not many weeks before the feminine element of our rides began to dwindle in numbers. The rising sun is not a spectacle which can be looked upon very frequently with a pleasing result by eyes that were made for coquetry. Accordingly, we transferred the hour of our ride to shortly before sunset, and wound up with dinner and a dance.

At length, some evil genius suggested a progressive dinner. We started at one house with cock-tails, and there being nothing else, these were supplied copiously, sufficiently so, in fact, to affect several of the horses on the ride to the next house. The next course was soup, and being, by this time ravenous, we consumed large volumes of it. Then came a long trot, which left us decidedly the worse for our lack of temperance during the soup course. Fish came next, after which we trotted to the house where chicken and vegetables were served. The next period of jostling caused decided hostilities between the chicken and fish, which were in no way soothed by a salad.

About this time, one or two dropped out, but the remainder braved another shaking up, and passed the milestone marking

45

mango ice cream. By the time we reached coffee and cigars, two more horses were gone, and their former riders were following in a *calesa*. At the last house, an orchestra played for us to dance, but only a few copper-lined individuals made feeble efforts to respond.

One by one, we went slowly to our homes. It was the last of our rides, known ever afterwards in our regiment as "the indigestion party."

It was during our period of recuperation, when simple diet was in vogue, that we began to turn our attention toward economy in the kitchen. I had noticed that Ramon, the cook, was beginning to show signs of prosperity, which manifested itself in a habit of adorning himself much more elaborately than was his former custom. Among other things, he no longer wore his *chinelas* over bare feet, but had taken to socks. These were usually of a decidedly dazzling color, and in order not to lose their full effect, he pulled them up over the outside of his trouser legs, and fastened them in place by means of a large pair of bright blue garters. He had also acquired a new straw hat with a pink band, and appeared one morning with a fine-looking game cock, which he had evidently gotten for speculative purposes.

Every day, I gave Ramon a small sum of money with which to purchase fresh vegetables at the market. He would record these purchases in a notebook kept in the kitchen for the purpose, and return the remaining change to me.

Suspecting that he was making away with some of this money, I learned from independent sources the actual market price of the vegetables which the cook had been buying: I then went to the kitchen and took down the note-book from the nail where it was hanging to find that these articles had been set down as costing about three times as much as they should have. Ramon was eying me all the while from across the room, evidently with a view toward finding out just how far he could go with these prices without straining my credulity.

Without saying a word, I picked up the first handy missile, which happened to be a skillet, and sailed it past Ramon's head. Several pans, some potatoes, and a fresh coconut followed, as a pair of green-and-purple socks, supported by blue garters dodged behind chairs and disappeared back of the stove. I then turned toward the door, and strode pompously out.

Next day, I entered the kitchen, and after glaring at Ramon, walked to a box where he had been splitting kindling, and picked up a hatchet. With this in my hand, I approached the note-book, took it down from its nail, and examined the entries for the day. Prices had dropped to almost nothing.

I pondered for a few moments over the book, hung it back on the nail, replaced the hatchet, and walked out without a word. From that day on, we had the most economically run table in the regiment.

CHAPTER VII

Lublub - The Carabao that Charged

It was in September that I began to notice numerous large wicker cages crossing the plaza toward the market. Usually they were carried in pairs, dangling from the ends of a bamboo pole which rested on the shoulders of a native. I could see from the confused fluttering that they were crowded with large brown birds, but was unable to make out what kind they were. After wondering for a while, I sent Narciso to stop the next *hombre* who came by with a cage, and bring him to me. For the next two hours Narciso squatted on his heels in front of the house, occasionally smoking one of the cigarettes which Tucker had found missing from his table drawer, and thinking about nothing at all.

Finally he came in, followed by a brown and wrinkled individual with bright eyes and skin like an alligator's. The old fellow grinned, showing the ragged stumps of several teeth, blackened from betel nut chewing, and held up his cage full of birds. He informed us that he was very old, and came from far away, that the birds were hard to catch, that he was very wise and could catch them in the rice fields at night with a light and a net, that other Filipinos could not catch these because they had no net, that he was extremely poor and wanted some rice, that he would sell the birds for two and a half cents apiece, and that he liked American soldiers.

All the while, l was looking at the birds. They had slender

wings, short tails and plump bodies, long straight beaks, and a peculiar idiotic expression due to their eyes being set almost in the tops of their heads. At last the snipe had made their long annual flight across the sea from China, and the rice fields would be a paradise for the hunter.

After learning from the old fellow that the native name for snipe was *magok*, I gave him a media peseta, and he very artfully stood with his back to me and handed Narciso his two smallest birds. This occasioned an outburst from the latter, which I quieted by saying that I preferred young birds, and accepted the rather scrawny specimens. When the old man had waddled off sufficiently far not to observe and set me down as an imbecile, I released the captives. They rose with a squawk and a flutter, twisted and zigzagged crazily from side to side, swung into the wind, climbed high above the town, and headed toward the rice swamps to the south. I had never hunted snipe, but realized from their aerial antics that they would make a difficult target for one accustomed only to the straight flight of quail.

Whitson, who lived about a quarter of a mile away, had been talking of snipe hunting ever since our arrival, so I wrote a note telling him that the birds were here. As Narciso was busy, I gave the note to Hollingsworth's boy, Kuroki, and told him to take it to Whitson. Kuroki, who had been so named by Hollingsworth, due to his resemblance to a Japanese admiral, took the letter and started off. Half an hour later he came shuffling back with the note and said, "Sir, no can give latter to *teniente* Whitson. Cornelio, his *muchacho*, tell me he sleep."

After expressing my views of Kuroki's intelligence, I directed him to give the letter to Cornelio, and to tell Cornelio to give it to his master when he awoke.

Another half hour passed, and Kuroki again appeared, hot and, dusty, still bearing the letter. He wiped his forehead with the tail of his shirt and murmured disappointedly, "Sir, no can give to Cornelio. When me go back, Cornelio he sleep."

My next remarks were such as I rarely find occasion to use, but sufficed to send the letter to its proper destination.

At dawn next morning, I called up to Whitson's window. He came down, shot gun in hand, and together we climbed into a *tar-*

tanilla, one of those ridiculous-looking covered vehicles balanced on two wheels and drawn by a scrawny pony. Its driver wore a sky-blue cheese cloth shirt and a pair of drawers, and was cramped into the narrow space allotted him between the dashboard and the front of the vehicle. As we climbed in by the iron step which protruded behind, our weight tilted the *tartanilla* backward and almost lifted the pony from the ground, as he stood humped up in the middle with his ears back and his tail switching.

We sat facing each other on the two seats, which ran longitudinally, crowded our legs into the narrow space between them, and waited impatiently while horse and driver settled their differences of opinion.

Like nearly all of his race, our driver was totally lacking in any sympathy for, or understanding of, a horse. When the bewildered animal refused to go, he swung his whip through the air near its ears, uttered Visayan profanity, and jerked violently on the reins. This usually made him back. Finally the pony, having tried everything else, started off, and was rewarded by a heavy beating. No wonder the poor creature balked, for he knew from bitter experience that the whip always followed his start, and he ceased to balk only when the jerking of the iron bit against his jaw became insufferable.

When the sun rose, we were rattling along the white coral road which led southward. The morning mist still hung over the peaks on our right, and from time to time, as the road neared the beach, we could peep through openings in the foliage and see the sails of fishing vessels silhouetted against the flaming eastern sky.

Huge coconut palms lifted their heads high above the nipa  shacks which nestled in the shade at their feet, their long fronds glistening with dew and trembling gently in the morning breeze. Very few of them bore coconuts, the blossoming stems, which would normally have borne fruit, having been cut off, and the sap allowed to drip into joints of bamboo. This cider-like sap ferments quickly, and mixed with a bitter bark, forms the tuba which mellows the Visayan during his evening hours.

Tuba-gatherers were running up and down the trees by means of the notches cut for their toes, emptying the sap into long bamboo buckets which hung from their shoulders, and cutting thin slices from the ends of the stems with their sharp bolos, to keep the juice running.

The palms were full of these men, half naked and climbing with the agility of apes. Everywhere resounded a hollow, ringing noise, as the tuba men pounded on the recently emptied bamboo joints with the backs of their bolos to loosen the sediment which had collected at the bottom since their last visit.

Below, among the nipa-thatched houses, children were playing, and women in bright colors were weaving at hand looms, preparing food, suckling babies, or gossiping at the roadside. Men were making fish traps, training fighting cocks or else squatting on their heels in that incomparable state of mental relaxation known as "just settin'."

At Mambaling they were having a fiesta - they usually were. Bamboo arches, decorated with palm fronds and colored streamers spanned the road. Tissue paper lanterns hung from every window, and red-and-white flags fluttered from poles, or hung from strings stretched between houses. In an open space, a crowd was eagerly watching the roasting of a pig in a heated pit and the filling of several huge earthenware jars with tuba. Members of a string band were collecting under a recently-erected shed and tuning their instruments.

By the time we had passed Mambaling, we were on the lookout for someone who might direct us to the best hunting grounds. Whitson pointed out a likely-looking individual, who, from the amount of mud on his legs, appeared recently to have come from the rice-paddies. Recalling that the old snipe-vendor of the previous day had called the birds *magok*, I confronted the mud-spattered native with the results of my recent struggles to learn his language.

"*Sabut ca hain na mga magok?*" I said, with considerable effort. "*Wa, na ca sabut,*" he replied, gravely shaking his head, and leaving me in an argument with Whitson as to whether the man meant that he didn't know where any snipe were, or that he had no idea what I was talking about.

The next two natives answered in similar fashion, so we began to experiment by putting our guns up to our shoulders and simply saying, "Magok," in a questioning sort of a way. All shook their heads except one, who said "boom, boom," and nodded knowingly as though he had made a brilliant discovery.

Whitson, who was enjoying my efforts thoroughly, suggested that perhaps the whole trouble lay in the fact that snipe might be magok where the old man came from, but were probably something else at the next barrio.

One of the first things to be learned in the Philippines is the use of pantomime to fill the gaps in your very limited vocabulary. I knew the word for bird, so stopped an old *tao* with a cock under his arm and repeated my original question, substituting *langam* for *magok*.

"Oo," he replied, "Yes, many birds."

"Et ung, langam," - "This bird," I added, and attempted to impersonate a snipe.

I was familiar with the conventional ways in which our moving picture actors "register" joy, sorrow, starvation on the desert, or love at first sight, but how to "register" jack snipe for the moment

had me puzzled. My eyes fell upon a long straw, which I picked up and stuck into my mouth by way of a beak. I then made a motion indicative of removing my eyes and placing them in the top of my head. "*Et ung langam,*" I repeated, uttered the rasping squawk of a snipe, and, flapping my arms like wings went cavorting down the road, zigzagging from side to side and squawking wildly at every zig-zag.

The native, after eying me solemnly and thoughtfully for some time, appeared to comprehend. "*Lublub,*" he said.

"Where are the *lublub*?" I asked.

He puckered his protruding lips together into the form of a snout, which he twisted over toward the left side of his face. "Over there beyond the bamboo there are many."

We looked in the direction indicated by his mouth, and through a rift in the feathery green foliage could see a network of little dikes with the intervening grass-green muddy rectangles of an old rice field. We took our guns and made for the field. Several carabaos were wading about, knee-deep in the mud and water, and grazing on tufts of wet grass. Two of them had large white herons perching on their backs and pecking occasionally at the ticks and other insects which they found there. In a corner of the field, an old bull was wallowing in a mud hole and slime At times, nothing but his nose would appear above the ooze and slime. Then his great back would stick out, and he would pile mud on it with a sweep of his long flat horns, and disappear again in the gray sticky mass.

A carabao unaccustomed to white men is usually a very unpleasant creature to encounter, so by way of protection, we took a couple of eight-year-old naked boys into the field with us. As we passed near the mud hole, the old carabao looked up and saw us, but continued to wallow. Fifty yards further on, the wind blew our scent to him. Whatever the scent of a white man may be, it has an electrifying effect on a carabao. No sooner had a breath of the tainted air reached the old bull, than his head rose, his great bulk stiffened, and he sprang from the wallow. For a moment he stood facing us, his head high, his horns extending back toward his powerful shoulders, his nostrils dilated and sniffing the air.

He remained this way for a moment, and then the dripping, muddy mass started for us at a trot, his nose still high in the air, and his large feet leaving the soft ground with a sucking sound.

At fifty yards, he broke into a run, throwing up great hunks of mud from his hoofs as he came on.

I could see his eyes plainly now. They wore a peculiar expression of combined terror and rage, as though the creature felt that death would overtake it at once unless it could destroy the object of its dread.

There was no tree nor fence within reach, and my little twenty-gauge shot gun loaded with bird shot was no weapon to stop this monster. When the bull was twenty-five yards away, my eight-year -old native boy stepped in front of me, threw a small clod at the beast and yelled "Ooey! Ooey!" The animal turned tail at once and galloped off sheepishly toward his wallow. The other carabaos did not charge, but came within about seventy-five yards and stood with their noses in the air pointing us like so many bird dogs.

Just as the Hindu gains from childhood a close understanding of the elephant, so does the Filipino grow up in a spirit of intimacy with the carabao. It is no uncommon sight to see an old bull grazing peacefully in the sun with a native child sitting half asleep on his back, or a baby playing about in perfect safety almost under the hoofs of one of these powerful animals. And the same beast which ruminates contentedly while small brown children climb overt its back, tug at its ears and twist its tail, will often charge with mad fury at every white man whose detested odor is carried to his nostrils.

Accompanied by a native, the snipe hunter is safe from the attacks of carabaos, but without someone to introduce, and vouch for him, he is very apt to be charged, if among animals which have not become accustomed to white men.

Occasionally, when alone, I have stopped the too-near approach of a truculent looking carabao by throwing clods toward him and yelling "Ooey! Ooey!" in native fashion. This has usually left him standing nose in air, apparently convinced that I was a common creature with a most uncommon and inexplicably vile aroma.

Whitson and I had separated, and were following opposite edges of the field. Numerous borings where the birds had probed the soft mud for worms showed that snipe were about in abundance. Soon they began to fly up with their rasping "ska-ape," zigzag crazily and fly off. The first ones all flew off, for standing on a slippery rice dike six inches wide, with deep mud on both sides and a carabao eying you from behind, is not conducive to good marksmanship at a target which keeps changing its mind concerning the direction of its flight. When my gun went off, I usually found myself with one foot frantically pawing the air, in an effort to keep from losing my balance and sliding down the dike into the deep mud alongside.

My only satisfaction was that whenever I heard Whitson fire, he fired twice in rapid succession. I smiled inwardly every time I hear, the *bang, bang,* on the other side of the field. "If he had gotten the bird with his first barrel," I reflected, "he would not have fired the second, and having missed once, another and more difficult shot would not be likely to touch a feather." But my gloating was short-lived, for a series of single shots soon showed me that Whitson had gotten into form, and I knew him to be a good shot.

While I was wondering if I would ever learn to shoot these aerial acrobats, I recalled the advice of an old snipe hunter. "When the bird says `escape,' wait until you have said `I'll be damned if you escape' and then shoot." I decided to try his method.

I heard a flutter and a derisive "*Ska-a-pe.*" I damned myself vociferously in the event of his success, and then let my gun off with a bang. Down came the snipe. The next three followed in like fashion. I found that by the time I got through damning myself, the birds were much further away than those at which I had been previously firing, that their flight was much steadier, and that they had begun to swing toward the wind on the arc of a circle. This made their shooting only little more difficult than that of quail in open country.

At noon, we rested in the shade of some palms, and refreshed ourselves with cool draughts of the juice from freshly gathered green coconuts. When we counted our birds, there were forty-two.

CHAPTER VIII

The "Mermaid" - A Nest of Babies - Withered Fingers - Rough Weather

Another Sunday rolled around to break the monotony of weekday routine. Down by the wharf, rolling lazily at its moorings, was the Mermaid, the 25 foot cruising motor boat which I had brought with me from San Francisco. Time and again, it had taken me out over the horizon, while I watched the towers of San Nicolas church sink slowly out of sight. It had hovered in crystal-clear water over beautiful gardens, where brightly-colored fishes played in schools, and blue star fish stood out like jewels against a bottom of glistening sand. It had landed me on tiny green islands, where coconut palms skirted the clean white beach, and parrots and monkeys chattered in the tangled jungle beyond. It had bucked and plunged among turbulent white-caps, dripping and glistening with spray. On balmy tropical nights, it had parted the velvet surface of quiet bays, leaving a wake of ripples for the moonlight to

dance upon. Such was the little craft upon which my thoughts dwelt, as I breakfasted on a luscious mango that Sunday morning.

"Who would like to take an all-day spin in the Mermaid?" I asked. Weaver, who was always ready for anything, piped up at once. The others had already made their arrangements for the day. Tucker and Clement were bound for the cock fight, and James was to beguile the time with a fair damsel who had come by the last transport. Perhaps there were those who envied him.

At the dock, Isiong, the Mermaid's "crew", was sitting on his heels - his usual pastime. He had had three predecessors. The first allowed someone to steal the anchor, the second was put in jail too often to be useful, and the third had social proclivities. This last boy was the worst nuisance of them all, and was named Foss.

Whenever there was a fiesta of unusual splendor (a very frequent occurrence), Rosario would come to me with tears in his eyes, enlist my sympathies with some heart-rending tale of calamity, and, ask for leave to attend the burial of some near and dear relative. When his mother had died, I had sympathized to the extent of several pesos and a couple of days leave. Then came several more family tragedies, coinciding strangely with the dates of fiestas, and exhausting the supply of near and dear relatives. While the death of his mother had become a very regrettable event, the second demise of that estimable lady was a little too much for me,

and I told her grieving son that I was through with him. As he left, he pointed to a particularly wild-looking heathen squatting near the water and said, "Good boy, pretty soon you like."

The object referred to had a shock of hair which would have done credit to a comic-opera pirate, and wore a green undershirt and the scanty remains of a pair of white cotton trousers. I found him totally impervious to English, but in a mixture of poor Spanish and Visayan, conveyed to him the fact that he was my *launchero*, that he must clean the boat thoroughly, and stay there until I came back.

I went home, and for a day or two forgot all about him. When I came I found the Mermaid beautifully washed and polished, the brass mountings shining like a mirror, and the boy perched on the stern, gazing contemplatively at the horizon and holding a fishing line between his toes. This was Isiong.

I made no arrangements with him, but once a day allowed him to come up to the house to get some rice and fish, which seemed to satisfy him perfectly, for he was always on hand, and kept the boat spotless and shining. After I had possessed him for several months, I gave him the sum of five pesos, which he promptly invested in an air gun and a gold tooth. Thereafter he varied the monotony of sitting on his heels, with the pastime of shooting sparrows off of the end of the dock. When he wished to look particularly imposing, he would get some metal polish, shine up the gold tooth, and slip it over the outside of one of his front fangs.

Weaver and I climbed into the little craft. Isiong gave the fly-wheel a twirl, and we were off. We glided out of the harbor, rounded the light house, passed the low-lying coral rocks at the southern end of Maktan, and headed for Olango, a little island to the east of it. I had never been to Olango. Despite its proximity to Cebú, there was little intercourse between them. Its inhabitants fished, raised a few *camotes* and a little corn, but saw little of the outside world.

We followed the eastern shore, looking for a landing place, and musing over what we might find beyond the thirty-foot wall of coral which held back the sea. For centuries, the waves had eaten into this rock, carving it into fantastic shapes and undermining it with dark grottoes. Gnarled and stunted trees lined the edges of the wall, while their naked roots hanging down over the water, writhed, twisted and clawed for crevices in the rock. Altogether, the island had a weird forbidding look. It was such a place as the childish imagination might picture as the haunt of some dragon or other fabulous and uncanny creature.

Opposite a break in the wall of rock, where the ground sloped back from a narrow beach, we dropped anchor in fifteen feet of water, over a fairy garden of growing coral. On one side of the boat, we looked down upon fishes slowly and gracefully gliding about in their limpid element. Blue and green parrot fish went among the coral branches just as their feathered namesakes were doing among the boughs on shore. Sea turkeys moved their weird shapes with a peculiar fluttering of their painted fins, and a Moorish idol drifted by, his long plume waving gracefully above his back. On the other side of the boat, the bottom dropped off like a cliff to unknown depths.

In a few moments, we were out of our clothes and in the water, swimming about in the warm sunshine, diving, splashing and enjoying ourselves thoroughly. By lunch time, we had developed the appetites of a couple of young bears, and dug ravenously into a basket of tempting delicacies which our cook, Ramon, had prepared for us.

Then came the heavy after-dinner languor which settles over every living thing in the tropics at the siesta hour. We obeyed its call, stretched ourselves out under the shade of the awning and, rocked by a gentle swell, forgot the world for an hour.

When we awoke a strong breeze had sprung up, and the Mermaid was jerking at her moorings. We went ashore, crossed a beach covered with sea urchins, anemones and colored shells, and climbed the little slope to the main level of the island.

The land was flat and brush-covered, but full of clearings and *camote* patches, the otherwise monotonous skyline being broken by graceful coconut palms, and the dark green domes of mango trees. In the edge of a large clearing I saw what appeared to be a little shack. Upon approaching it, we found that it was a thatched roof supported by four stout posts, with a heavily-woven mat attached by its corners to the posts, sagging down in the middle, and forming a sort of hanging nest.

Whatever was in the nest was alive, for it kept bobbing up and down and moving in a most animated fashion. Peculiar bulges would appear near the bottom, gradually work half way up the side, and then roll suddenly down again. What was in it? Who put it there, and why didn't it jump out? We wondered.

When we peered over the edge, we found to our surprise, four Filipino babies of assorted sizes, all less than a year old. Two of them were trying to climb out. They would get a little over half way up, cling frantically to the ever-steepening sides and then come sliding and sprawling down into the protesting mass of arms and legs below. I could easily imagine what an ear-splitting chorus would have arisen from white babies under similar circumstances, but in this land where almost every woman over fourteen keeps on hand a child of less than a year, I scarcely ever remember having heard the cry of a baby.

While we were wondering over the parentage of this brood, and the cause of its being here, we caught sight of several native women some distance away working in a *camote* patch. Evidently some genius among them had contrived this means of safely and conveniently disposing of their offspring during the busy hours. From the apparent age of this contrivance, it had doubtless served a like purpose for several 'years, and with next season's crop of *camotes*, might be counted on to care for next season's crop of babies.

We wandered about for an hour or so, and then started back for the beach. On our way there, we stopped a native carrying a basket of unusually luscious-looking mangos, and were on the point of purchasing them, when something about the hombres appearance arrested our attention. He had a peculiar expression about the eyes, like a lion in the zoo, gazing disinterestedly at a group of curious spectators. Whether it was a slight raising and drawing together of his eyebrows, a thickening of the upper portions of his cheeks, something about the shape of his nose, a drooping of the outer corners of the eyes, or what, it is hard to say, but the general appearance of a bored lion was the result.

I had heard doctors speak of this expression, and began to look the man over. The hand in which he held out a large ripe mango was scaly. The other was behind him, but I slipped to one side to get a view of it. What I saw, was the withered stumps of what had once been fingers. -- Leprosy!

When we returned to the Mermaid, white-caps were blowing from the waves, and the boat rolling and plunging. We had scarcely started the engine when we saw a dark fin protruding from the water not thirty yards away, and exactly where we had been swimming.

I turned the steering-wheel over to Isiong and reached for my rifle, while Weaver whipped out a .45 revolver and we both opened fire. By a stroke of luck, I was able to plant a high-powered soft-nosed bullet in the shark's spine at the base of the fin, and the creature slowly began to roll over on his side. Isiong swung the boat around, and headed straight for the shark while Weaver and I climbed to the bow. As we passed over the fish's body, I let him have another .33 bullet just back of the head, while Weaver's .45 made a couple of more holes in him.

We turned the Mermaid again, and grabbed a boat-hook, eager

to secure our trophy, but with the tossing and plunging of the craft, managed to do nothing more than lose the boat-hook overboard. By the time we got the boat over the carcass again, it was gradually sinking out of reach. To jump into the water and fasten a rope to it, would have been an easy matter, but thoughts of another shark deterred us, and our prize slowly disappeared in the blood-stained water. It was a huge creature, and we agreed at the time that it must have been at least twenty-feet long. Even after making the proper allowances for the fact that it got away, that we didn't measure it, and that no one else saw it, our fish still remained a big one.

It was sundown when a tide-rip caught us at the northern end of Maktan. A mill-race current from the mouth of the harbor, came head on into the heavy waves that piled in from the east, stirring up a sea which threatened to send the Mermaid to the bottom.

Our boat was tossed, jerked and buffeted by huge masses of dark water, which kept shooting up like sharp hillocks all around us. At one moment we would be caught by one of these pyramids of water and lifted high into the air on its crest. Then it would seem to vanish from beneath our keel, and we would find ourselves in a deep hole with a wall of brine all around us.

A bottle of kerosene rolled from under one of the seats and smashed against the opposite side of the boat. An empty gasoline can toppled against the flywheel, was thrown into the air and clattered down near Isiong's head, scaring him half to death. Weaver picked it up, assured himself that it had no holes in it and remarked, "This wouldn't be half bad as a life preserver, would it?" However, he didn't need it.

After supper that night, we lingered for a time over some old Spanish port and cigars and amused ourselves with my boy. He knew practically no English when I got him, and in order that he might develop a style of speech embodying individuality and distinction, we always addressed him in the most stilted combination of long words that we could think of. Naturally, he took this for the highest form of speech, and struggled violently to acquire it.

"Narciso, have you administered sustenance to the diminutive canine?" Weaver asked, looking at the bulging puppy which was waddling about the room.

"Yezzir," he replied, "he eas replete."

"It is my august desire, Narciso, that you replenish our goblets with the elixir" I said, and held out my glass to the gurgling decanter. This was a new expression, and I could see that he was trying to memorize it. Tucker's glass was the next to be empty. Narciso approached him gravely with the decanter.

"Sir," he said, "you wish the gobble of the elicker?" Tucker did.

James handled him a phonograph record and told him to "invoke the muse." When he was half way through winding the instrument, there was a peculiar indigestion noise inside of it, the crank turned limply, and nothing would induce it to play.

In spite of good training, Narciso had evidently gotten some of his English from outside sources. "The muse," he said, "iss goddam."

CHAPTER IX

The Oil Cannon - The Dead Rooster Wins - Anting-anting

Clement had just joined us from Manila, and had never seen a Visayan cock fight. 1 had not seen one for three weeks, so we decided to go together. Just why we settled on the one at Naga, I don't remember. Possibly because we had heard that there was such a place, and had never been there before.

As we drove past Talisay, several strings of fire crackers sputtered in the main street, followed by the clanging of the church bell, and the booming of three bamboo cannon. The native cannoneer was leaning over this noisy implement and after blowing kerosene violently into the touch-hole, which partly vaporized it, he stuck a match to the vent and set off the explosive vapor with a bang. We watched one hombre blow until his eyes bulged and he became dizzy, whereupon another human bellows took his place and produced a violent explosion after every blow.

This seemed to be the signal for the start of a grotesque religious procession which followed a tissue-paper float toward the church. Seated on the float was a tinseled statue of the Virgin with yellow hair and a long blue robe. Eight natives in red trousers and green shirts were pulling it along with a rope, and behind the saintly wagon walked a couple of clowns about eight feet high. Their heads were made of papier maché, had staring eyes and an idiotic smile showing several irregular and lonesome-looking teeth. A pair of brown legs protruded from the bottom of each, and native eyes blinked from holes along the waist lines of their yellow-robed bodies.

I once asked a priest why he permitted supposedly religious affairs to take such absurd forms. "It makes them go to church," he said. "They are children, and all children love a circus. After we get them into church, then we can preach doctrine to them, but we have to make the church interesting to them in order to get them to come, in the first place." Maybe be was right.

It was still early when we reached Naga. A superb array of crowing roosters was picketed near its buttressed old church. Clement scanned them with a critical eye. "Plenty of good material for a fight when the padre gets through", he said. "However," he added, "I believe our South Carolina birds could clean them up.

I wouldn't mind if I had a couple with me today."

While we were talking, the crowd began streaming out of the church. By some strange process of reasoning, it has become an established custom that no man can enter a church with his head covered and no woman with her head bare. Consequently, most of the women wore their little church-veils of black lace or embroidered piña over their glossy hair. Others simply spread handkerchiefs over the tops of their heads and stuck them in their belts as they came outside.

By ten o'clock, the entire male population of Naga had drifted over to the *bulangan, tartenillas, carretelas,* carabao carts and other vehicles were hitched near the entrance. Large kettles of rice and fish were being cooked over open fires, and the smell of roasting pig filled our nostrils. Half a dozen little stands were scattered about, tended by women, from whom food, betel nuts, blue eyeglasses, tuba, or kerosene lamps might be bought, after the usual preliminary haggling over the price. The purchasing process was always the same:

"What is the price of this?"

"Two pesos."

"Too much."

"No, Senor, it is very good."

"What is your lowest price, your ultimo precio?"

"One peso and a half."

"I don't want it."

"Ah! Senor, it is a very fine one. There are others, but none so good as this."

"No good, I don't want it."

"What will you give?"

"Forty centavos."

"It is impossible, Señor. It cost me more than a peso, but I will sell it to you for one peso." The prospective purchaser turns on his heel and starts away; He is called back. "Sixty-five centavos, Señor." The purchaser returns.

"I will give you fifty-five centavos."

"Very well, Señor," and both are satisfied.

We moved for a while among the crowd in front of the *bulangan*, and then entered. Inside there was a broad open shed, filled with a garrulous throng of men and roosters. It was like the paddock of a race track where the contestants received their last touching up before the contest.

Scores of cocks were crowing themselves hoarse, and straining at their strings in vain attempts to reach their taunting neighbors. Men were grooming their birds, smoothing out their feathers, massaging their leg and wing muscles and giving them the finishing touches of a long period of training. Others were moving about, eying, feeling and discussing the relative merits of the chickens and preparing to bet their last peseta on the one which most caught their fancy.

Two of the pit officials came into the shed and at once became the center of attention. They moved about deliberately, talked to a few of the chicken owners and settled on the cocks for the first fight. This started a wild, excited flood of discussion relative to which would win. But the discussions were short-lived and it was soon agreed that one of the prospective fighters was far better than the other. This would never do. Violent difference of opinion was essential to the sport, so two other cocks were selected.

This proved a happier choice. The discussion grew into an uproar. Each group gathered around its champion and scoffed at the backers of the other. An old hombre who had been whetting a number of murderous-looking slashers chose a curved blade of appropriate size and shape for each bird, and carefully adjusted the weapon to the bird's left leg.

I watched this operation closely. The rooster's natural spurs had been clipped off. A sort of leather boot was placed around his leg, and the scythe-like blade attached to this, so that it projected just below the stub of the old spur. It was fastened on by means of a waxed string and the process of winding it on at precisely the proper angle, with exactly the right number of windings called forth grave deliberations and the deft touches of a professional. A protecting scabbard was then slipped over the gaff for the time being, so that he would not injure himself or anyone handling him before the fight started.

I asked the old fellow why he always selected the left foot for the slashers instead of the right and he said, "A chicken is left-footed. He always strides first with his left spur. If I should put the blade on his right foot, he would cut his left leg off with it."

The crowd now began to drift through an inner gate into the main part of the pit. On one side of the arena a sort of platform was partitioned off by a railing and on this were chairs for such *distinguidos* as might lend éclat to the gathering by their presence. Apparently Clement and I were regarded as being of the éclat variety, for a couple of natives were yanked out of the center of the ringside row, and we were bowed to the chairs which they had vacated. On the other sides of the pit were the "bleachers" for less distinguished visitors. These were rows of bamboo poles arranged in tiers, where the ordinary *tao* might root and cheer the victor.

Inside of the ring was gathered a grave-looking group of officials. The judge, who was the main dignitary, was arrayed in a costume appropriate to the importance of his position. A canary-colored shirt with broad, red stripes hung over the outside of his spotless white trousers. A huge pith helmet, suggestive of an Indian tiger-hunt, adorned his head and his feet were thrust into chinelas of purple plush.

But all these were mere matters of adornment. By far the most important function of the judge was to see with the eye of an eagle, and be free from the optical illusions which so often befog the vision of those unfortunates who bet on the wrong rooster. His decisions must be based upon eyesight so keen that no one could raise a protesting voice. This he had provided for, and at the beginning of each fight, he carefully opened a small hardwood box, and adjusted to his eyes with conspicuous care a large pair of bright green goggles. Thus equipped, he was generally admitted to possess the infallible eye.

On opposite sides of the ring stood the contestants, carefully guarded by their owners, pecking from time to time in the sand, and occasionally crowing defiantly at their opponents.

Then came the betting. Several men began to rush around the ring yelling excitedly to the crowd. They called out the names of the cocks, shouted the betting odds, and exhorted everyone to lay his money on the fight. At once, silver pesos and bills began to fall into the ring, each man shouting as he threw down his money, the name or color of his bird.

While Clement was in the act of backing his judgment with a five-peso bill, a foppish native on my right, with a ring and a new straw hat offered advice on the outcome of the fight. *"Mayyo og manok, ang maitum,"* he said. "The black is a fine chicken."

This decided me at once. I had received "sure tips" at the race-track, so promptly laid my two pesos on the red rooster. That is to say, I threw them into the ring and tried to say "red rooster" in Visayan, to the infinite disgust of my advisor, whom I later saw doing the same thing.

No one seemed to pay any attention to what was said by the bettors, but before the fight began, all the money was collected and placed in several piles on the ground in one corner of the ring.

This being done, the two handlers approached each other, rooster in hand at the center of the ring. Two paces apart, they stopped and held out their chickens, one red, and the other a glossy black. Already the feathers on their necks began to rise, as each thrust his head forward and glared at his antagonist.

The eyes of the red cock were then covered by the hand of his handler, and the other bird allowed to give him one hard peck on top of the head. A similar courtesy was then bestowed upon the red cock, who retaliated by landing his beak as heavily as possible on the pate of his enemy. This customary formality being over, the handlers stepped back three paces, placed the birds on the ground and slipped the scabbards from their slashers. Then, at a signal from the judge, the cocks were released.

At first they approached each other warily in little zigzags, their necks outstretched, their bodies low, and their wings ready. Then, after a little rush, they stopped, beak to beak, and poised themselves for the spring. In a moment, both were in the air, striking viciously as they met. Again they squared off, and again came together in a whirl of wings, clicking steel, and flying feath-

ers. This time when they settled down, one of the black cock's wings hung a trifle lower than the other, and a few red drops trickled down his feathers and made a dark stain on the ground.

There was a roar from the crowd at the first sight of blood. "Kill him! Kill him!" "The red!" "Blood, blood, look at the blood!"

When they rose again, the red was above. As the black struggled into the air, his wounded wing weakened, and he half spun round, so that his feet and gaff no longer interposed between his vitals and the thirsting weapon of his antagonist. With a powerful stroke, the red cock drove the two-edged, razor-like blade deep into his breast, as a deafening shout rose from the wildly excited crowd.

It had all happened in a moment. Less than a minute before, two superb cocks, who for months had been trained for the arena, had met to measure steel. Now the exultant crow of the victor rose over a gasping
heap of bloody feathers. In my sympathy for the vanquished cock, I had quite forgotten my financial investment. The men who had

collected the money had already begun to circulate among the crowd, each with a hat full of silver and bills. They appeared to be handing out the money indiscriminately as they moved about. Finally one came to me and presented me with four pesos, though how in the world he knew that I had bet two pesos on the red rooster is still a mystery. There is something uncanny about the way these people keep track of the betting. Money seems to be thrown into the ring entirely unnoticed, hundreds of pesos are often bet on each fight, the odds frequently change during the betting, yet not one figure is put on paper, and never have I heard complaint of the distribution of the winnings. I have never seen a white man who could understand it, nor a native who could explain it.

One of the fights that day was won by a dead rooster. He was struck down by a vital thrust from the other, but the gaff stuck firmly in his breast. His antagonist fluttered wildly in an effort to free himself, thinking, no doubt, that his enemy had some strange unrooster-like way of holding him by the leg. Finally, with a frantic effort, he freed himself, and ran to the other side of the ring, bewildered and frightened by what had happened. He was brought back by the judges and placed in front of his dying opponent. With all the strength he had left, the latter feebly raised his head, glared defiance, and showed that his fighting spirit was still alive. The other had enough. The little hack- feathers just back of his comb were raised in admission of defeat, and he ran away again.

The head of the other slowly settled back to the ground. He gasped as the blood surged up into his throat, his eyes became glazed, and he was still. The judge carefully eyed the two through his green goggles, and announced as the victor the one who had died game.

Before long, an old Chinaman, dressed in dark purple, walked slowly into the ring and took his seat at a table which seemed to have been reserved for his use. Evidently he was a personage. His skin was like dark parchment, seamed and deeply wrinkled. His jaw was square, his forehead broad, and beneath it shone a pair of deep set inscrutable eyes, which seemed to take in everything but give no inkling of the profound thoughts which were going on behind them,. It was Si Sip, a wealthy merchant, a highly respected Celestial, and a notorious devotee of the bulangan. He nodded with grave dignity toward the judge, placed a large bag of money on the table, sized up with a glance the cocks which were being brought in for the next fight and promptly laid a hundred pesos on one of them.

During the frenzied yells which rose from the natives during the fight, I watched the face of this heathen philosopher. Not a muscle changed. One of the cocks was cut down, still Si Sip sat like a graven image, nothing in his expression betraying in the slightest degree whether his rooster had won or lost.

As the sport continued, he made no movement other than to shove a pile of money to one end of the table before each fight, and point to one of the cocks. Sometimes several hundred pesos would come back; sometimes nothing at all; but whatever were the emotions which dwelt within the brain of this old Chinaman, they never percolated through his face.

Later on, I got to talking to him, and remarked that he probably looked upon cock-fighting more as a business venture than as a source of amusement. To my surprise, however, he assured me that as far as the money was concerned, he always came out about even in the long run, but it was the fun and excitement of the thing that induced him to come and bet.

The noise in the outer shed, where we had entered, kept growing as the morning wore on, and Clement and I strolled out to stretch our legs and have a look at anything that might be going on. The hubbub came from a garrulous group standing around two huge earthenware jars full of tuba, which was fast disappearing at one centavo a dipperful, the dipper being half a coconut shell.

Clement called my attention to a native who was bringing out a cock which had just lost his fight. The bird which he had trained, petted, and caressed for months, had lost money for the hombre and the bond which has held them together was gone. The cock, though badly gashed, was still alive, and struggled a little when his master started to remove the gaff. Without giving the poor creature another thought, the native pulled out a knife, cut off its leg, kicked the feebly struggling cock out of the way, and went about unwinding the string from the severed leg.

While we were standing there, a particularly bibulous hombre staggered over and held up a waxed string for our inspection. "Anting-anting," he said, "A charm." He went on to explain that he had just bought it from an old man for a peso, and that the old man had gotten it from a great priest. Whenever a rooster's gaff was tied on with that charmed string, he told us, the gaff would always find its way to the heart of the other chicken. It had been proved last Sunday. Now he would enter his manok and bet all of his money. He hoped that we would lend him some more, so that he might bet a great deal and become rich. Twenty minutes later, he came out from the pit with an empty pocket, a dead rooster, and murder in his eye. He made straight for an old Filipino who was sitting quietly near one of the jars of tuba. He rushed angrily up to the old man, shook his fist violently and started delivering himself of an angry tirade. The old fellow held up one finger and spoke a few words in a low voice. The infuriated look vanished from the other's face, he replied in a genial sort of a way and went off looking entirely satisfied. I followed him and asked why he had lost and what the old man had told him.

"*Seguro!*" he said. "Other hombre have two anting-anting string. Old man, he say next Sunday sell me three."

Many a poor devil has suffered from this superstition about the anting-anting. During the insurrection, anting-anting shirts were sold by some of the native priests with the promise that they would make the wearers invulnerable. In fact, they were shown to be bullet-proof by firing at them with blank cartridges. Only an anting-anting bullet would pierce one of them. Another shirt of this variety would make its possessor invisible to enemies, although entirely visible to friends. During the insurrection, a clever merchant let it be known that one of these shirts had been stolen by an American soldier. It was announced that at twelve o'clock on a certain day, this hostile soldier was going to walk down the beach in front of a village where arms were being collected, and under cover of his magic shirt, spy upon the *insurrectos* there. At noon, the whole village had turned out, and every eye was vainly focused upon the beach. The soldier was invisible, and the shirt's charm established beyond question. By twelve-thirty, the local supply of anting-anting shirts was sold out.

Chapter X

Hunting on Leyte - Admiral O'Brien - The Hospitable Presidente - The Laughing Jackass.

It was on a bright Sunday morning in September that Tucker, James, and I, each with a broad smile of satisfaction spread all over his countenance, left Cebú on board the quartermaster launch, *Mobile*, in charge of that illustrious seaman, "Admiral" O'Brien. Williams and Whitener, who were stationed with our 3rd Battalion at Ormoc, had frequently invited us over for a little hunting trip on the island of Leyte, and at last we were off with ten days leave and nothing on our minds but amusement.

Cebú is about as hot a place as can be found this side of the brimstone lake, and this was a particularly hot day for Cebú, so we were doubly glad to get away. We welcomed the cool breeze which sprung up after we got started, lolled under the shade of a canvas awning, and listened to how "the Admiral" had weathered various and sundry typhoons. When we were well outside the harbor, Tucker tried to sleep, James tried to shoot gulls with his pistol, and I tried to catch a shark by trolling. Tucker was the only one of us who had any degree of success.

In the early afternoon, the Mobile passed the three little Camote Islands and headed toward the rugged, saw-tooth skyline of Leyte. A couple of porpoises kept abreast of our bow for miles, and schools of flying fish fluttered to safety as our boat glided quietly along through the water.

We reached Ormoc an hour before sundown. A dozen officers and their families all in white, were sitting out on their porches, or strolling up and down the row of quarters and dropping in on their neighbors to drink a cup of tea, or empty a tinkling glass of iced scotch and soda, and pass the time of day. It was good to see them all again, and they welcomed us with warm hospitality. That night they gave us a hop, which wound up in the wee hours with a Virginia reel, which nearly shook their nipa club off its foundations.

Next morning we rose early (the morning after a hop is always early), and with Williams and Whitener, got back on the Mobile. It seemed early, too, for "Admiral" O'Brien. He had every appearance of having passed through a typhoon the night before. Maybe he had.

Whitener, who had evidently been reading some book on African safaris, said he had made all arrangements for the trip. "A white man in the tropics, he said "must always travel like a gentleman." We did. We were provided with every unnecessary article which the whims of the most fastidious "gentleman in the country" might call for. We had a soldier for a cook; folding cots and mattresses to sleep on; *muchachos* to smooth out our sheets, pull off our shoes, and, serve our breakfast; provisions enough for a continuous banquet; and several *cargadores* to form a nucleus around which to gather the "safari" which we expected to have when we struck inland.

Our launch headed southward and several hours later dumped our imposing pile of impedimenta on the beach at Hilongus, op-

posite the ruins of an old Spanish church which showed the scars of fighting during the insurrection. Game was abundant. Our plunder was scarcely ashore, when snipe, curlew, plover and doves began to tumble to our guns.

Whitener, meanwhile, had gone to the village and made arrangements for our stay in a place suitable for gentlemen traveling in the tropics. A new house had just been completed and the family had moved in the day before. Whitener, with the aid of our retinue, moved them out again, and managed somehow to convey to them that they were much honored to have us select their house as the best in the village wherein to rest our noble selves.

Before turning in that night, Tucker and I went down to the

beach for a swim. The night was overcast and still, and the unrippled water looked dark as ink as we slipped out of our clothing and crossed the beach. We threw ourselves in with a splash, and to our great surprise, the darkness suddenly vanished and we each became the center of a cloud of weird flickering light. Every ripple that we made, went out like a greenish-white ring of fire, and every splash threw up a handful of luminous pearls.

The air and water were of the same temperature, both balmy and soft. It was like swimming in some fairyland of liquid moonlight, each limb, as it swept in its stroke, lighting up like a long flame. When we were still, the inky blackness closed in around us, only to burst again into a flood of light at our slightest move. From time to time, a large fish was frightened by our approach and went out to sea looking like a rocket in the phosphorescent water. It was a sight worth remembering.

The next day, which was a rainy one, found us at Cubcub in search of duck, which we were told abounded there, and we were not disappointed. A couple of little ponds afforded some excellent flight shooting; and later we had good sport in the rice fields where numerous duck were feeding. Most of them were of a variety not unlike the mallard, while others resembled cinnamon teal. Snipe were so plentiful that after each of us had gotten a fair bag, we stopped shooting at them. Even the beautiful painted snipe were there in great numbers.

At about two o'clock, we assembled in a small shack near the rice fields to get out of the rain and eat the lunch which one of our boys had brought along. A native in the shack was rubbing two pieces of bamboo together, and when I asked him what he was doing, he replied, "Bog-id." I watched him, to find out what "bog-id" meant, and saw that he was making a fire in this primitive fashion, for the purpose of lighting his large home-made cigar. He took a flat piece of bamboo about ten inches long and an inch and a half broad, and with his bolo, cut a narrow longitudinal groove on the underside until it barely came through the top. Then he took a similar piece and gave it a sharp edge. Holding the first piece down with his toes, he sawed across it with the second at the place where the groove came through. The groove would shave off little pieces from the sharp edge, and the friction would ignite these. It took the hombre a little less than two minutes to shape his sticks with a bolo and get his cigar lighted. After a little practice, I found that I, too, could bog-id.

After a swim and a supper of roast duck from our Dutch oven and snipe broiled over a bed of live coals, it was decided that we should go down to the beach to Bato next day, stay overnight there, and strike inland into the mountains on the following day.

James volunteered to get the necessary *cargadores* for the trip. Next morning, when we saw how he went about it, most of us felt rather dubious of his success. He first presented the jefe de policia with a number of ducks and snipe, and told him how greatly we had all enjoyed our stay in his town. Then he asked him if he would be so kind as to help us get some cargadores, provided it did not inconvenience him. James had had little to do with Filipinos, and did not realize that to reward a native who had done nothing for him, and tell him that we would feel greatly indebted to him if he could favor us with a little of his time, was the quickest way to lose his respect and a hopeless method of getting cargadores.

An hour and a half later, we had seen nothing of him; so I sent a boy to his house, directing him to come at once. Not seeing James, he shambled up to me with a condescending grin, and announced in Spanish that there were no in Hilongus, that our plunder was too heavy for anyone to want to carry it, and that no one cared particularly about accompanying us anyway. So saying, he turned on his heel, and started to shamble off, probably to finish eating some of the game which James had given him.

He had scarcely taken a step when I exploded with every Spanish epithet that I knew, asking him how he dared to come to me, an Americano, with such a pack of lies, and telling him that I intended to have those cargadores and that I had no idea of waiting very long for them. Instantly the attitude of the *jefe* became one of profound respect. He snatched off his hat, stood with his heels together, and when my supply of Spanish gave out, set off down the street at a run. In less than half an hour, he was back with fourteen cargadores and profuse apologies for not having gotten them sooner. Several of them, he told us, he had taken from the jail, and we might use these as long as we liked without pay, and set them free when we were through with them.

After supper, Whitener and I went down to the market place, which was very large for so small a town. Evidently Bato was a supply-station for the mountain people of a large district. As an indication of this, we noticed a number of bamboo joints with *bejuco* loops, each joint containing one or two days rations of rice and putrid-smelling fish for the mountain hombre to use on his homeward journey.

The market was arranged in two very broad streets, with booths or *tiendas* along the sides, and a double row of women down the center, each squatting by a smoky coconut-oil lamp with her wares spread out on a mat in front of her. They all had about the same things to sell. I stopped beside one who seemed typical, and took note of her stock. She had an earthenware jar of tuba with a coconut-shell dipper to drink out of, a few packages of cooked rice tied up in *burre* palm leaves, two small lumps of indigo, half a dozen betel nuts, a piece of asphoedita, some red and some russet-colored bananas, a pair of glass earrings, a handful of chocolate beans, several ears of roasted corn, a dead (very dead) fish, and a bolt of striped calico. She was suckling a week-old baby, smoking a huge cigar, and haggling with an old fisherman over the price of two betel nuts and a drink of tuba.

We drifted into the best-looking *tienda* we could find, and sat down. The two women running it were Tagalogs who in some way had strayed down there from Luzon. They were very anxious to give a dance, a *baile*, in our honor. In the *tienda* we found a native who had been machinist on a small inter-island boat, and who spoke very good Spanish. For fear that we might not be fully impressed with his fluency, he talked incessantly all the time we were there. During part of the time that we were listening to him, he informed us that the town had a bakery run by two Japs, where all the bread was baked. Every morning at exactly the same hour, *segun el custombre del pueblo*, His Honor the Presidente would put on his official trousers, tuck in the tail of his shirt, (a thing done only on occasions of ceremony), and inspect the bakery. Needless to say, "*segun el custombre del pueblo*" the bakery was always found dirty, and always left so.

Wherever we went, half the town was at our heels, watching as though we were the greatest of curiosities. A white man is a rare sight in this neck of the woods. In our wanderings, we picked up a string "orchestra" which really played very well on their home-made instruments. We attached this orchestra to the procession and had it follow us to the *casa municipal* where it serenaded us while curious eyes peered in through the windows and watched us all go to bed. A couple of well-directed basins full of water improved the privacy of our retiring.

Bright and early next morning, our caravan struck inland, bound for the mountain *burrio* of Anahawan. Whitener and I went ahead with our guide, and got some good duck shooting as we followed a mountain stream. At the request of some natives, we also shot some white cockatoos which were destroying the corn. The cargadores later appeared to enjoy eating these birds so much that we tried them ourselves, and found them delicious.

What a Visayan finds wildly amusing about a wounded crow, I have never been able to understand, but it is evidently a source of unending mirth to him. Whitener shot at one of these birds, and it flew off with one leg hanging down, apparently broken. Our guide saw it, and burst into uproarious laughter. He roared until his voice was all gone, and then leaned up against the trunk of a tree from sheer exhaustion and shook limply. Several times he half recovered himself, pointed in the direction the bird had taken and again collapsed against the tree in a convulsive outburst of mirth.

Half an hour later, we met a native coming down the trail with a pig on his shoulder shaded by a green parasol. He was stopped and regaled with all the particulars concerning the wounded "Wok" by our guide, who by way of illustration drew up one leg, hopped on the other, and flapped his arms like wings. The other hombre, after recovering from his first spasms of laughter, set down the pig and went through the same pantomime, to the infinite delight and amusement of our guide. From then on, everyone we passed was left roaring over this humorous classic, which was invariably illustrated by the hopping and flopping of our guide.

It took nearly five hours to reach Anahawan. The day was hot, and the going hard for the *cargadores*, and we had to halt frequently to give them a breathing spell. Whenever a halt was made in a coconut grove, we would send a boy up for a green coconut, and refresh ourselves with its delicious juice. No matter how hot the sun may be shining on a growing coconut, its juice is always cool and refreshing.

At Anahawan, we got hold of its chief potentate, the teniente of the barrio, and in our smattering of Visayan, managed to tell him what we wanted. The little bamboo school house was turned over to us, and the teniente sent over some stools, a lamp, and something resembling a table.

The only other real dignitary in town was the *jefe de policia*. He constituted, in himself, the entire police force of the barrio and did well to call himself chief. Hearing of our arrival, he attired himself in his robes of state - a khaki cap, probably discarded by some soldier years before, a striped shirt, and a pair of drawers. He then paid his official respects to the *barrio's* guests, and attached himself to Williams. When Williams wanted to smoke, the jefe would rush around to his house, get some tobacco and make a cigar; when Williams went hunting and wished someone to carry his game, again the jefe would come to the front; when Williams expressed the august desire to sit down, forthwith the *jefe de policia* would place a stool most conveniently for the satisfaction of his wish. I have never seen such an admiring satellite, or useful public servant.

None of us had hunted wild boar, and we learned from the natives that the only way to catch sight of one was to sit in a tree near one of their runways. James and I each got an hombre to show us where to go. Mine was so monkeylike that I almost suspected a simian bar sinister. He was very small, and had a funny little round head set low on his shoulders. His nose was flat, and a pair of inquisitive eyes peered out from a wrinkled and leathery face. His long arms dangled as he walked, and his big toes stood out almost at right angles to the others. With these he showed remarkable prehensile ability. Barnum could make a fortune out of him. I never learned his name. For a while we referred to him as the prehistoric Lilienthal man, which soon degenerated into "Lil." Lil carried a bolo nearly as long as he was, and could cut his way through a thicket with remarkable skill and speed. The only trouble was that the hole which he cut for himself was never quite large enough for me. When we finally got to a suitable tree, this monkey-like creature was up it in a minute, and in less than five minutes had made a comfortable platform for me to sit on. When I was properly settled, he climbed to the top of the tree, perched himself on its upper branches and held on with his toes.

Toward the cool of the evening the sleeping forest began to come to life. A bird with the prolonged liquid trill of a *veery* began singing in a tree full of orchids a few rods away. Another made peculiar sounds like the driving of a hardwood stake with a small hammer. A troupe of monkeys passed chattering as they jumped from branch to branch. A couple of brilliant orioles began fluttering about and a beautiful bird with scarlet and green plumage began searching for insects among the bushes. Then, from a point several hundred yards behind me, came sudden loud outbursts of wild laughter, like the guffawing which might have followed some coarse jest in a half-drunken lumber camp.

I looked in disgust at the heathen, who had kept me sitting all afternoon in a tree so near such an orgy. "What in the devil is that?" I asked. "Langam," he said, flapping his arms - "bird. It is a calao."

I could scarcely believe my ears until I later saw one of these creatures in the act of making this uncanny laughter. He was a sort of toucan as big as a rooster, black with white markings. His tremendous beak was a brilliant red, and its base extended well

back over the top of his head, forming a sort of hollow sounding-box. He was a strange creature. The soldiers call him "the laughing jackass" or "habla bird."

Several wild hogs rooted their way through the dense undergrowth not thirty yards from my tree, but none came in sight. I was all on edge every time one came by, but not once did I catch a glimpse of anything to shoot at.

James reported much the same luck. He had seen three very large hogs come out into the open behind him, but found himself in such a position that he was unable to turn around slowly without making enough noise to frighten them, nor could he shift his position quickly without falling out of the tree. Hence no hog.

On my way home, I stopped at the shack of the teniente, who had just brought in some fresh tuba. I took my first drink of this popular Visayan beverage, and immediately associated with the many unpalatable articles which are said to derive their popularity from "an acquired taste." It is fairly certain, however, that had I indulged in several drinks of it, I should soon have become incapable of tasting anything.

The others, who had hunted birds, came in well laden with game. Among other things, they had a number of "baud," large wood pigeons as big as crows.

The next day James and I perched and meditated as before, but beyond hearing a few pigs moving through the brush, our meditations were uninterrupted. Tucker decided he would take it easy and not go out with the others. He lounged about for a while, and then, having nothing else to do, took his rifle and wandered up the mountain with no particular object in view. He had not learned the only possible way to see a pig, so he strolled along puffing at a cigarette, humming a tune, and thinking about something back at home. Suddenly his thoughts took a tremendous jump from Virginia to Leyte, and he found that he had almost stumbled upon a fine boar, who seemed too much engrossed in rooting something edible out of the ground to notice anything else. Just as Tucker's gun reached his shoulder, the pig came to with a jolt, let out a couple of "woof-woofs," and started off like an express train. He had gone scarcely ten paces, however, when a bullet from the Springfield rolled him over. That night we had spare ribs for supper, but James and I didn't enjoy them.

With fresh mountain *cargadores*, it took us a little over three hours to get back to Bató next day. The migratory spirit was upon us, and we decided to put to sea at once. We located a large sailing *banka* to our liking, but the tide was out and would not be in for five hours, and the *banka* was on a mud-flat two hundred yards from shore. The natives told us that it would be impossible to get the *banka* off before high tide, and thought it most unnatural that anyone should be in that inexplicable stage of mind called a hurry. It was with open-eyed wonderment that the whole town turned out to see us take about fifty men, drag the *banka* bodily over the flat, and set sail. The very idea of anyone's not being willing to wait for the tide!

The *presidente* waved us good-bye, and was all broken up over our leaving. He had been much honored, he said, by the visit of the "Americanos distinguidos," and begged us at least to spend the

night. As a token of his esteem, he had arranged to provide each of us with one of the belles of the town during our stay. He could not understand our declining his offer, which he considered the height of hospitality and good form.

When our *banka* spread its matting sail to the wind, we had no idea where we were going, a fact which in no way disturbed us, but rather added a touch of pleasurable speculation to the trip. Pretty soon it began to rain. There was no shelter on board, so we all took off our clothes and put them under a box to keep them dry, and then sat singing like a bunch of mermaids until the shower was over.

Shortly before dark, we approached an island which we liked the looks of, so we landed. As our boat neared shore, six *bankas* put out from the other side of the island in evident haste. We found later that they had been dynamiting fish with stolen dynamite, and thought we were after them. The *presidente* of Matarlan, a village on the Leyte coast nearby, had previously sent word to them to stop their illegal fishing; but since his police had no fire arms, and the fishermen had threatened to blow up anyone who molested them, the *presidente* forgot about the affair entirely.

Our little island was named, Kamigao. It was only a few acres in area, and was covered with coconut palms. A white lighthouse, tended by two Tagalogs, stood on one end opposite a reef, and about fifty fishermen lived in a tiny nipa *barrio* shaded by the palms.

To our surprise, we encountered eleven Moros on the island, who had come all the way from Zamboanga in their *vintas*. They were Samals, "men of the sea." They live in villages built over the water along little coves and estuaries; and their *vintas*, with carved bows and colored sails, skim the water before every monsoon. They smuggle, slip away with the wives and daughters of careless natives along the coast, take anything that is not nailed down, and lead a free, happy, enviable and piratical existence.

The contrast between these Moros and the Visayans was very marked. We had grown accustomed to a diffident lack of assurance in the demeanor of the former, but there was none of this about the Moro. The moment we landed, without any preliminary peeping from behind trees or waiting to be sent for, the Moros walked boldly up, looked us in the eyes like men, and sent forward their chief, who greeted us with his only English word, "Hello."

We went around to their camp, where their *vintas* were pulled up on the sand and a lot of fish drying in the sun. We knew a great deal about those fish before seeing them or talking about them. They had four boats, and the bow of each was a work of art in wood-carving. Nearly every Moro, however barbarous he may appear in every other respect, has the instinct for creating beautiful designs in wood and metal. His boat and his weapon are the two things dearest to him and he spares no pains decorating them.

The lighthouse was selected as our resting-place for the night, and our plunder moved in. As it is a well-known fact that a Moro considers it on all occasions good form to kill a few Christians, and since he will risk his life to get firearms, we came to the conclusion that we had better keep a guard on for the night. The others all agreed, but when night came they were all too sleepy and decided to "take a chance." Consequently, I spent the night with my weather eye open, considering it better to lose a night`s sleep than to risk waking up in Sharon's ferry-boat. As it turned out, the Moros slept as soundly as anyone.

The next morning, Whitener and I took a stroll around the island. Near the Moro camp, we shot some sort of a sea bird, and gave it to one of the Moros, thinking he would be glad to have it to eat. He replied by telling us that he didn't know us, and would not accept our food for fear of being poisoned. We retorted by saying that whenever we disliked anyone we shot him. Poisoning was too much trouble. Even with this assurance, I doubt very much if he ever ate the bird.

Before the sun was very high, our stuff has all been loaded on the *banka*, and Tucker, who was nursing a slightly injured foot, sailed with it for Matarlan. James went with him, as Williams suggested, to get expert advice on pig-shooting.

The rest of us got another banka, cruised around for a couple of days and wound up at Matarlan. By the time we had gotten our possessions lined up on the beach, and had a plunge in the water, a tiny white speck showed up on the blue horizon. It was the "Admiral," come to take us back in the Mobile, with his twinkling eye, his genial laugh, his typhoons and his red nose.

CHAPTER XI

The Wokwok - Ichabod – Scandal

The "States mail" had failed to bring any answers to our letters of three months ago, and a few were beginning to dread its arrival. So often of late it had brought little note beginning, "I am so anxious for you to be one of the first to hear of our engagement. John and I are so happy - I know you will just love him when you meet him. He's such a dear." One of our number whose slightly wilted affections had been completely revived by a rainy season in the tropics had received a lot of these notes, and had actually come to look upon such missives with real merriment. This mail brought him two, and he called Narciso and ordered a Scotch and soda with plenty of ice in it to drink to the health of John - poor John.

Narciso came back with the beverage but no ice. Apparently the ice plant was out of order, and the ice box empty. The boy placed the drink on the table and announced, "Hombre no put ice in arctic region dees moneeng."

Narciso was looking a little seedy, and was doctoring himself for a headache according to the usual native custom. In fact, he had slightly improved upon the method of his uneducated brethren; for where the untutored *tao* of the country normally pasted scraps of banana leaf on his temples, Narciso had a couple of pieces of newspaper the size of poker chips glued to his. I later informed him that the paper had greater virtue if it bore colored pictures, and thereafter he appeared adorned with excerpts from the comic supplement of our Sunday papers. He assured me that he found it far more efficacious, and that several of his friends had also profited by this artistic treatment.

A few hours after the arrival of the mail, we received our copy of a semi-occasional paper, the Cebú Chronicle, or "Barnacle" as it was usually called. We read in it a confirmation of all the news which we had just found in our home papers, and the additional announcement that there was to be an eclipse of the sun at 12:30 the next day. With a house full of superstitious boys, this news presented great possibilities.

The Visayans have an evil spirit, a sort of goblin bird, which goes by the name of *wokwok*. It sucks their blood at night, it eats their children, it walks through the streets and leaves cholera wherever it steps. Sometimes it takes the form of an old woman and works evil magic; but you can always tell when an old hag is a *wokwok* by looking under her arms. If she has a deep hole in one of her armpits, she is one of these dreaded creatures.

When the sun is high, many a native will laugh about the *wokwok* with an air of superior incredulity; but when night comes with its weird sounds and mysterious shadows, the same native will keep a light burning in his house until dawn and shudder at the mere mention of this blood-lusting specter.

Among the measures adopted for keeping him away, the most effective so far discovered is the placing of an "egg-plant" in the front window. A little shrub is set in a pot or box, and an egg-shell, from which the contents have been removed, is slipped over the end of every twig. So far as it is known, no wokwok has ever been seen in a house provided with one of these plants.

On the day of the eclipse, we had just sat down to luncheon, when I called in all the boys and made the announcement that I had seen the wokwok flying through the sky, and that he was going to eat up the sun. A row of broad smiles greeted this announcement. Martin was particularly amused. "No got *wokwok*," he said. The others said nothing, but evidently scouted the idea.

I sent for a candle, smoked half a dozen pieces of broken glass, and sent the boys out still smiling, to look at the sun. When they were outside, we all went to the front window to watch them. Martin was the first to raise his glass. Through the smoked surface, he could see the shining disc of the sun, and to his horror, found that a distinct bite bad been taken out of its rim. The smile froze on his face, and he turned an anxious look at the others, whose expressions by this time confirmed his fears. They spoke together in anxious whispers, and looked again. The bite was larger. Terror was on every face. One of them gasped something about Santa Maria, there was the tinkling of broken glass on the ground, and six frantic boys stampeded across the plaza and into the church, their shirt tails standing out straight behind them as they ran. While Ramon, the cook, was serving the rest of the meal, we taxed our ingenuity to keep him from looking out at the sun or finding out what direful things were happening to it.

Ramon had very recently been punished for a gentle little habit he had of picking chickens alive. He said their feathers came out more easily, and apparently the poor creature's cries of pain in no way ruffled his state of perfect composure. He had been cautioned against this piece of barbarity, and upon a repetition of the offense, we had suited the punishment to the crime, and dragged him across the kitchen by the hair.

Another mishap had recently befallen Ramon as the result of our boy Faustina's having brought a new and strange creature into our household. This creature was Ichabod, a long-legged, scrawny-necked bittern, with a six-inch murderous-looking weapon by way of a beak. Ichabod had been snared somewhere in the swamps, and now, with one wing clipped, strolled up and down the *azotea* on the end of a long string. Every day, we gave him a couple of handfuls of minnows, which he gobbled up at once, sending a succession of little bulges running, down his neck, like so many mice chasing each other along a string.

After we had him a couple of weeks, he bit his string in two, and disappeared, to turn up several days later next door, sedately following an old turkey hen along with her brood. He was a treacherous creature, and while apparently in the best of moods, he would often strike in a half spearing, half biting fashion with his beak, and almost take a chunk out of whoever happened to be within reach.

One day, while I was sitting behind a screen near one of the windows, I saw Ramon giving his rooster a last bit of training and exercise before taking him to the *bulangan* next day. As he gave the bird a final rub-down, his eye lit on Ichabod, who was standing on one leg with his neck drawn in and concealed somewhere along the feathers about his shoulders. Everything about him depicted boredom and lack of energy.

Ramon looked carefully around, and after assuring himself that he was unobserved, slipped the rooster up on the edge of the *azotea*, and slunk back out of sight to watch the result.

Seeing this ungainly bird before him, the cock flew at him at once, and knocked him sprawling upon his back, his wings flapping and his long legs kicking in a ludicrous attempt to get straightened out. With an awkward effort, the bittern shuffled back to his feet, while the rooster squared off with ruffled feathers, ready to flatten him out again.

Ichabod presented the most incensed picture of outraged dignity I have ever seen. He drew himself up, turned his head on one side, and out of one eye, glared at his assailant with a look of infinite contempt and scorn. Then, with a movement like lightning, he reached out two feet of neck, caught the offender's whole head in his beak, shut down on it like a nut-cracker, and began to shake. There was a shrill squawk of terror, a violent fluttering, and Ramon's rooster disappeared over the garden wall. He must have kept going, for I never saw him again. Ichabod, meanwhile had drawn up one leg, settled his head back upon his shoulders, and lapsed again into dreamy meditation.

Not many days later, while we were enjoying one of Ramon's salads of *obud*, the delicious nut-flavored bud from the top of a coconut palm, there blew in from Guimeras no less a personage than Hornsby Evans. He had just been transferred to the regiment, and was to enliven our household by becoming a member of it. Wherever Hornsby was, something had to stir. He usually did the stirring himself.

"Any scandal in the regiment?" he asked after a week without hearing of any. Naturally we told him no.

"Let's start some Saturday," he suggested. We asked for particulars.

"Well," he said, "if each bachelor can kidnap somebody's attractive young wife without the knowledge of her husband, I will charter Smith-Bell's steam launch and we'll have a scandal party."

On the appointed day, each of the victims boarded the launch at 5:30 in the afternoon "to chaperon a little surprise party." Under various pretenses they had all been induced to maintain the utmost secrecy regarding their destination, even from the husbands. They were scarcely aboard, when all realized that there was something queer about this party which they were "chaperoning," but by that time the gang plank was in, and the boat in motion.

We landed our captives at Kawit, the almost unused quarantine station on a little island at the mouth of the harbor. Most of us went there regularly every Thursday with Pat Rafferty, the Collector of Customs, in the customs launch for a swim. It was an ideal place for the purpose, with dressing rooms, fresh water showers, and a high place to dive from. Bathing costumes had been arranged for, and we had no trouble inducing our fair ones to take a swim.

While we were swimming, some fishermen paddled up in a large *beroto* shaped from a single log and steadied by bamboo outriggers. Near the remains of the old Spanish watch tower, they lowered a wooden anchor weighted with stones, and began to fish. The smallest minnow is always acceptable to a native fisherman, and these were apparently after small fry which would have fled in terror at the approach of any such monster as a sardine. Their catch was to become *guinemos*, that horrible mixture of whole minnows and a little salt, which, after several days' exposure to the sun, effectively prevents you from smelling the pigs and many other malodorous things about the market places.

Their fishing outfit consisted of a jelly-fish the size of a pumpkin, a closely-woven dip net, and a bucket. There is a kind of minnow in these waters which for some reason seems to take great delight in congregating in the hollow globe of the jelly-fish, and is apparently unharmed by its poison. Schools of these were playing about the boat, and the natives were having great luck. They would lower the jelly-fish into the water, and wait patiently until a dozen or so minnows found their way into his hollow interior. Then they would slip the net under him, empty his inhabitants into the bucket, and set him down again to refill. They got about a quart of these small fry while we were having our swim. After dark they were joined by a dozen other *beroto*-loads of natives who speared squid by torchlight.

It was only when the swim was over and that ravenous feeling which always follows a plunge had come over us, that some of our captives began to allude to their fast-approaching dinner hours, and mention the alarm which their husbands might feel at their disappearance. But husband and dinner hour notwithstanding, the launch was under our orders and didn't move. Fried chicken, and sandwiches, deviled eggs, ham, salad and coconut cake were brought ashore. A tub of ice packed around bottles of ginger ale and San Miguel beer was placed beside us, and we feasted. Night came, Japanese lanterns were hung on the mooring-posts of the broad hardwood dock, a native string orchestra struck up dance music, and the *baile* commenced.

It was considerably after ten that night when I escorted my fair charge to her home and stood prepared to drop her and run. As we approached the house, the sounds of singing and revelry came from within. At the top of the steps, the open door revealed all of the "alarmed" husbands sitting around a decanter, playing poker, and making merry.

I had scarcely taken in what was going on, when an offended little voice piped up beside me: "Bob, you heartless wretch, how could you be amusing yourself this way, when you didn't know but what I had been killed.'" Bob laughed heartily, and the whole bunch began to sing, "High, ho! The rolling river."

CHAPTER XII

Frosty Air – Cavorting with the Elephant – Mango Maria

A Year had passed, almost without our knowing it. Time slips by rapidly in the tropics with little to mark its flight. A period of daily showers, a stretch of clear weather, and spring, summer, autumn and winter have come and gone.

We had all started alike, full of physical energy, eager for violent exercise and possessed of an inward feeling of superiority over indolent neighbors. At first, we could scarcely get enough boxing, wrestling, running and hand ball. By and by, however, our exercises took a milder form. An occasional game of tennis, a swim at Kawit, and a daily ride took care of our surplus vigor, and kept us sufficiently trim. People around us appeared less and less lazy. In fact, we even began to wonder how some of them became so energetic. There came a feeling of restfulness and satisfaction, of care-free and luxurious irresponsibility; all of our little worries and perplexities blew away with the monsoon, and the spirit of the East was upon us.

The months drifted by, and we awoke one hot morning to realize that it was Christmas. It was "Mango" Maria who first greeted us with a bright "Mayree Kressmus" and brought, as a present, a basket of fruit. In the basket were mangos, pineapples, chicos, and yellowish-green lakatan bananas with their translucent custard-like interior. Maria had been coming almost every morning for almost a year, and we had always bought our mangos from her. It was thus that she had acquired the "mango" prefix to her name. She was well formed and always neat, and this morning she wore a new dress and a fresh *pañuelo* [handkerchief] of bright yellow *jusi*. She could scarcely contain herself with delight when we gave her, in return for her present, an old mirror in a white frame.

When she was gone, Tucker scratched his head and looked a little worried. "I've missed too many boats," he said. "It's time for me to be going back to Virginia. Mango Maria actually looked pretty this morning, prettier than a native ever can be. When a man begins to see pretty Filipino girls, it's time for him to go home."

Around the corner from us on *calle* Magallanes, an old German had felt the Christmas spirit, and had decorated his shop window in real Yuletide fashion. A little fur-robed figure of Santa Claus was sitting in a sled drawn by reindeer across a field of fluffy, white cotton, and flakes of the same substance were pasted all over the window in mimicry of a snowstorm.

On that broiling tropical day, it was a most incongruous sight. A withering sun was shining directly upon the almost perspiring red-faced figure in the sled, and a group of boys with naked brown legs were looking in at the window and wondering what it all represented. One of them was explaining, "It is San Nicolas. He makes it rain cotton for the Americanos." But his statement was promptly disputed by another who felt much better informed; "No," he said, "It is not cotton. It is *sorbete* - sherbet. The Americanos eat it. It never rains sorbete in Cebú, so the Americanos make it in machines."

It was not without a touch of homesickness that I saw the chubby little figure in the reindeer sled, the tiny fir trees, the broad -chimneyed cottage and the cotton snow. Thoughts of frosty air, a blazing fire and a generous bowl of egg-nog began coursing through my mind. Frost, cheerful faces and egg-nog - somehow these seemed to haunt me and clamor for their share in the Yuletide.

I went home, and the dearth of that cheering beverage, the steamy atmosphere and those insistent little voices made it seem far from a real Christmas. But at last we found a way; and while the bells of San Nicolas church were clanging their loudest, five broadly-smiling young bachelors stood beside the frosted pipes of the cold storage room in the ice plant, and emptied a bowl of egg-nog with a hearty "Merry Christmas."

It was not long after this that a circus drifted in on a tramp steamer, and began to unload at the dock. It had been to Sydney and Melbourne, to Singapore and to Iloilo, and was wandering northward toward Manila, Nagasaki, Hong Kong, and Shanghai. I was first made aware of its presence in Cebú by coming home and finding a large Bengal tiger, with its feet on the railing, looking out of one of our front windows. James stuck his head out of the next window and called out "Come up and join us. We have a new pet. Her name is Jenny."

However much of a pet Jenny might be, I could not help entertaining the idea that she might accidentally sit down on a bee and blame me for it, so I stopped by my room and came into Jenny's presence with a high-powered rifle ready for any possible misunderstanding. Jenny's escort informed us with great glee that he had just visited a saloon across the street, where he had perched Jenny on the bar while he took a couple of drinks. "Seein' as there wasn't nobody back of the bar for me to pay when I got through," he added, "I had to leave without payin' nothin'. The same thing happened down in Iliolo and Singapore. I reckon Jenny has been worth a lot of money to me just that way."

Like everything else in the Orient, the unloading of the circus from the steamer was done backwards. First came the animals, which were brought up to the plaza and placed in the broiling sun, where the heat of their iron-barred cages started a bedlam of protesting roars from the inmates. The tent, which was to have sheltered them, was found under a cargo of rice which could not be removed until next day, so out of pity for the suffering beasts, we offered the shade of our garden for the menagerie - a thoroughly rash act.

We were immediately deluged with all the natives in town, and everything not nailed down was stolen from about the premises. They even tore down some of our vines to steal the strings they were trained upon. The two elephants promptly pulled up and ate a pretty grove of banana plants in one corner; and throughout the night, the two lions, six leopards, three tigers, five bears and one hyena were wide awake and vociferous. So were we.

The next morning, I went out into the garden with several biscuits for one of the elephants - the other was busy pushing heavily-loaded trace from the dock to the plaza. The first biscuit was eaten with the same relish which had been shown toward our banana plants, so I presented the big, rubber monster with the rest, which he took in his trunk and promptly stuffed into his mouth. Having no more, I turned and started away. I had scarcely taken a step, when I received a rough prod from behind, and looked over my shoulder to see the creature, with extended trunk, demanding more biscuits, and decidedly irritated at my meager offering. I started backing away, but this resulted only in the elephant catching up and giving me another decidedly rude and unappreciative prod with his proboscis. I tried reaching in my pockets and slowly backing at the same time, when the brute lifted his trunk, let out a horrible scream, and started for me.

Ten yards away was an old stone wall about as high as a man's head. According to the Spanish custom, the rounded top of the wall was covered with broken glass, set in concrete with the jagged edges protruding to prevent anyone from climbing over into the garden. Strangely enough, it had never entered the architect's mind that anyone would want to jump out of the garden to escape an elephant, an oversight for which I was violently condemning him at the time.

How I got over that wall without being cut all to pieces by the glass, I haven't the slightest idea; but I got over, and didn't stop to look around until I was inside the house next door. No doubt, anyone seeing me would have been forcibly reminded of Ramon's rooster after his encounter with Ichabod.

When I got back, one of the showmen was leaning up against the elephant limp with laughter. "Why, Pete wouldn't hurt anybody for anything in the world," he said. "He just wanted to play a little." However, during Pete's stay, I never crossed the garden without a large reserve supply of biscuits, and shall never try to amuse myself by romping with a playful elephant.

We had the ring master and the "Princess" in for tea, and very naturally received complimentary box seats at the performances. We deserved them. The Princess rode bareback on the white horse and jumped through tissue-paper rings, the strongest man in the world performed unheard of feats, the drunken sailor wandered in and won a bet with the ringmaster by riding the bucking mule backwards, the grotesquely-clipped poodle ran away with the trainer's whip and refused to bring it back until its owner had promised not to use it on him - all of the familiar old sights were there but two, the King of the Cannibal Isles, and the Wild Man of Borneo. These two gentlemen would have created little stir in Cebú.

The big tent was packed with a heterogeneous crowd. Americans, together with Britishers, Germans, Spaniards, and other Europeans filled the boxes on one side of the ring, while the other seats were crowded with natives of all sorts, mostly without their children, and Chinamen almost always with them.

Before this motley assembly, with its divergent ideas of what might be called amusing, a couple of clowns gave the most remarkable performance I have ever seen. They would face the boxes and get off some jest which set us all to laughing, followed by something which did not seem funny at all, but which would bring roars from every Chinaman present. Then they would make a crack in Visayan, another in Spanish, and again switch to English or Chinese. Every minute, their jokes and horseplay shifted to amuse a different nationality and a totally dissimilar sense of the ridiculous. A little trick, movement or gesture, which in no way whatever seemed possible of an amusing interpretation, often brought prolonged outbursts of uproarious laughter from the natives, while these would as frequently sit in silence and wonder why every white man was shaking with amusement. Behind those painted idiotic faces, lay a wonderful versatility of wit.

It was not without a feeling of relief that we said good-bye to the household tiger, the Princess and the frolicsome elephant. They had all been entertaining, but they kept us in a continuous state of speculation as to what any one of them might do next. When they were gone, we settled down again to our regular routine. Our work started with the sun and ended by noon, the siesta claimed us during the hottest hours, then came white uniforms, calling and tea, dinner, and a long evening which was bound to be interesting before it was over. In fact, the best part of the day was between midnight and bedtime.

However modern we may think most of our inventions, it nearly always turns out that some Chinaman has thought of them long before us. In the Philippines, where a sum of money placed in the hands of parents makes easy the road to matrimony, the Chinaman has long ago thought of trial marriage. Since the China-men are thrifty merchants, they nearly always had the wherewithal to acquire the girls who are most sought after, and since they are reputed to be the best of husbands, it is little wonder that they are unpopular among Filipino bachelors.

For a couple of weeks, we had not seen Mango Maria, and had begun to miss the very choice fruit which she always brought. Tucker, whose breakfast mango was not quite up to standard, asked his boy what had become of her.

"Chino, he buy," replied Martin.

"How much did he pay?" said Tucker.

"He pay seventy-five pesos, and he try. If he like; he keep and pay seventy-five more. If he no like, he bring back. Maria very fine girl, cost more than carabao."

A month later, I saw Maria in a dress of embroidered *piña* and a silk parasol, strutting down Magallanes street as though she owned it - "Chino, he like."

CHAPTER XIII

Mindanao - The Mosquito Feast - The Living Cloud

A month or so passed after the circus had left, and I again felt the migratory spirit and prepared for a trip in the Mermaid. I had heard so many weird yarns about Mindanao with its Moros and wild tribes, its tall mountains, its dark forests and its abundance of game that I could not resist a desire to go there and disappear for a few days in its jungles. I arranged for a ten-day hunting leave, but at the time, none of the bachelor officers of the regiment could so regulate their affairs as to get away. I tried the married officers, but was unable to prevail against the storm of protest from their wives, who seemed possessed with visions of widowhood. Unfortunately, they had all heard of the last motor boat which had started for Mindanao with two white men about six weeks before. The men had never been seen since, and the boat, stripped of all its brass fittings, had been found floating in the Sulu Sea. Consequently I decided to go alone.

It was four in the morning when, with Isiong at the wheel, the Mermaid cast off from the old quarter-master dock, and started on her voyage. The sky was evenly overcast with low, smooth clouds, and the day came with a monotonous grayness which seemed to subdue every color and give a leaden aspect to everything. The sea was calm and without a ripple, its velvety surface broken only by the wake of the Mermaid, and the occasional splash of a porpoise, as he rolled and floundered in his morning play. Large jelly-fish trailed their poisonous streamers behind them, and water snakes peered curiously at us as we glided by.

Presently, a stiff southeast wind sprang up, and the water became white-capped and choppy. Then big swells came piling in, and the Mermaid rolled and twisted in the trough of the sea. The boat was built for rough water, and would stand anything short of a typhoon, but cooking supper became nothing less than an athletic achievement. The little Premus oil-stove had to be wired to the flooring to keep it still. Then by sitting with my back against one side of the boat, and bracing my feet against the opposite seat, I managed to hold a skillet above the blue flame and prepare enough fried eggs, sliced bacon and batter-cakes to last us until the next meal. The boiling of a pot of chocolate followed, although a good deal of the beverage splashed out during the process.

By sunset the sky had cleared and the wind died down. Night came on with a rush and the Southern Cross appeared like a glittering jewel over our bow. There was no sight of land, no sound save the swish of the waves and the steady throb of the engine as we glided on in the darkness.

At length, the jagged coast of Mindanao began to loom up ahead, silhouetted against the ruddy glow of a forest fire in the mountains beyond. Lights twinkled through the darkness, and sounds began to float to us across the water. With a fiery V of phosphorescence at our bow, and a trail like the beam of a searchlight marking the path of our propeller, we swung round the northwestern corner of Mindanao, and at ten o'clock anchored over a sheltered reef near the shore.

The moon rose like a red ball behind the distant screen of smoke, lanterns glimmered against the blackness of the cliff, and the sound of music and of voices floated out over the water. I could hear the distant barking of a dog, the crowing of a gamecock, and the snorting of a school of porpoises as they played a little way out to sea. While the Mermaid slowly rocked to and fro at her anchor, all these sounds gradually blended themselves into a soothing melody, and I sank into a delightful sleep.

An early start next morning got me into Dapitan harbor by seven. An inter-island trading steamer was just weighing anchor as I went in. Its captain called to me from the bridge as we putputted by him.

"Hey, there! Where are you from?"

"Ran down from Cebú yesterday."

"The hell you did. In that little thing you're settin' in, with all them waves? Well, I'll be everlastingly damned! Not over twenty-five feet, is she?"

"Just twenty-five," I said.

Again the captain everlastingly damned himself, and forthwith steamed out of the harbor.

At Dapitan I found a company of native scout troops commanded by an officer named Wright. I had written him that I was coming, but since he was considerably off of the regular mail routes, I arrived some weeks ahead of my letter. He was just back from a little expedition in which he had been exploring a new trail across that corner of Mindanao. During the course of his explorations, the native detachment which he had along had twice been attacked by some of the wild tribes of that region, and Wright was very much elated over the way in which his scouts had driven off their assailants, inflicting considerable losses upon them.

Being out of touch with the rest of the world, and the only white man in that region, Wright had gradually acquired all the functions of one of those benevolent oriental potentates so common in literature and so rare in the Orient. Daily, the *presidente* and chief of police reported respectfully for orders. About once a week everyone having grievances and disputes came to accept Wright's judgments, and Dapitan was kept clean, happy, and fit to live in.

Wright had apparently planned to be away that day, for when he sent word to the kitchen that we would both be there for lunch, his boy announced that the cook had gone off, and later brought news that he could not be found at his house.

"Send for the chief of police," said Wright. That dignitary arrived about five minutes later.

"Where is my cook?"

"I do not know, Señor."

"Turn out all your police force and get him here in time to cook lunch."

"Yes, Señor," and without further ado on Wright's part, a delicious lunch was served.

My first aim was to get a good pair of boar's tusks to show Tucker when I got back to Cebú. Wright provided me with three of his men, a sergeant of police, a policeman, and a prisoner, and when lunch was over, we started up the sluggish stream which flows into Dapitan Bay. We were soon in good pig country, but I had learned that the pigs here were entirely nocturnal in their feeding, so spent the afternoon looking for likely feeding grounds. Finally, I discovered a fruit tree under which there were numerous pig tracks and by dark had left my men in a shack a mile away, and concealed myself on a big, flat rock fifteen yards from the tree, and so located that the breeze would carry my scent away from it.

With night, came the weird sounds of a tropical forest. The moon would not rise for an hour yet, and as I lay in that inky darkness, I began to think of various awful things which might happen. Suppose a big boar approached from the wrong side and took offense at my presence, or perhaps a thirty-five foot python should become interested in me. I recalled seeing the picture of one which was killed not fifty miles off, and which was found to have swallowed a whole deer.

Just as I was turning these delightful thoughts over in my mind, there was a flopping sort of a noise followed by the most horrible, blood-curdling shriek I have ever heard, it ended in a sort of hoarse gurgle, like something in terrible pain being slowly strangled. I nearly jumped out of my skin, and then grabbed my gun and tried to locate the sound. It came from the branches of the tree and was repeated by a dozen other voices, which shrieked like so many evil demons above me. There was a short silence, during which a large piece of fruit from the tree dropped near me with a thud, and then the shrieks were renewed. All the while, I was straining my eyes to catch a glimpse of one of these creatures against the sky. Finally, I saw several huge bats as large as turkey buzzards circle the tree and settle in its branches. The noises were nothing more than the celebration of these big fruit bats, or flying foxes, over having found a particularly good supply of food.

There was a long wait until moon-rise, and even then the shadow's made it difficult to see. There were a couple of patches of moonlight under the tree where I would be able to see a boar if one came, but when I pointed my gun toward them, I could not see the end of the barrel to aim. This I remedied by tearing off a strip of my white handkerchief and tying it around my gun barrel near the muzzle.

During the next two hours the rock that I was lying on got harder and harder, the dew settled chilly and dripped over everything, and the mosquitoes gathered for a feast. Nothing but the thought of Tucker and his exasperating luck kept me from leaving. Then came the sharp crack of a stick, the tearing sound of something being uprooted from the ground, a grunt and the crunching of heavy jaws. A big boar was coming down the hill, and feeding as he came.

Slowly he came on. It seemed an age. Then with several low

grunts, he walked within ten yards of where I lay, and began to feed under the fruit tree. So far I had never seen him, but could tell from the amount of noise he made, that he must be a big one. For half an hour, his great jaws crushed the tough fruit stones not fifteen yards away, while my eyes were glued to the two little patches of faint moonlight where lay my only hope of seeing him.

I dared not move an inch, for fear of alarming him, and realizing this, every mosquito in that part of Mindanao settled on my face and the back of my neck. I blinked my eyes, screwed my face up into knots, and tried to waggle my ears, but all to no purpose. The buzzing, bloodthirsty swarm continued its orgy.

Just as I was becoming almost frantic, a big, black shadow darkened one of the patches of moonlight, and I faintly made out the outline of the boar. The white strip of rag on my gun showed up against the dark body, a spurt of flame shot out, and a hoarse choking sound followed the report. I quickly pumped another cartridge into the chamber and waited. I could see nothing and hear nothing. If there were any mosquitoes, I did not feel them.

For five or six minutes I remained where I was, not caring to stir up a wounded boar in the dark. Then I began throwing stones at random near where I had last seen the animal, and hearing nothing, walked down and found him less than three paces from where he had been shot. He had been less than twenty paces away, and seven of the nine buck shot in my cartridge had struck him just back of the foreleg. Two had passed through his heart.

Early next morning, I took the trophy back to Dapitan and started down the coast in the Mermaid. We turned into the mouth of the Ilaya River, followed the little stream for ten miles through a dense, tangled forest, and tied up in a beautiful hunting ground of alternating woodland and waist-high grass. By noon next day, I had a deer, some ducks and a good string of wild pigeons, all of which I took back to Wright and spent the night in Dapitan.

I had found it rather irksome to keep an eye on the police sergeant, in order to see that he required the policeman to look after the prisoner, so when I returned to the hunting grounds I took only Isiong. Leaving him in charge of the boat, I walked about three miles from the river to look for deer feeding in the grass patches at sundown.

Having seen none, I started back at dark, after lighting a little lantern which I had been carrying on my belt. I had gone scarcely half a mile, when I heard a sound like the roar of a wind storm. It seemed very near, but I was surprised, and rather perplexed to find that not a breath of air was stirring. Suddenly, a living cloud swept over me, and I found myself almost smothered in a swarm of millions of locusts. I ran for a couple of hundred yards, but the blinding cloud kept sweeping over me. It occurred to me that it was the light which was attracting them, so I put it out, and finally freed myself of the swarm. Then I stopped to catch breath, and shake off the locusts which still clung to my hat and clothing.

There is little wonder that the Bible speaks of the coming of locusts to Egypt as a plague. When first hatched, the larvae are unable to fly, but hop along like a great army of grasshoppers, devouring everything green in their path. At this stage, the natives of whole towns turn out and drive them into trenches and pits, after which they collect them in sacks, roast and eat them. But if no locust-eating John the Baptist overtakes them, the larvae soon develop wings, and the devastating cloud begins its work of destruction. It sweeps over cultivated areas, and where green crops were flourishing in the morning, not a living thing can be found by night. It settles upon groves of fruit trees, stripping them of every leaf, and leaving the naked branches to blister and dry in the sun. Then it passes on and dies, leaving myriads of eggs to carry on the havoc next season.

It was not until I had passed through a strip of woods, and gone some distance beyond, that I ventured to relight my lantern. Meanwhile, it had grown overcast and very dark. About this time it dawned upon me that in escaping the locusts I had completely lost my bearings. I wandered about for some time trying to find something familiar, but there were no distinctive landmarks, and every open patch of grass looked like every other one. I knew that if I went north I would strike the river, but I had not brought my compass along, and it was too cloudy to get my bearings from the stars. I was seized with a wild impulse to walk fast - to run - and I knew that I was lost. Realizing this, I sat down to think it over, but neither landmark, watercourse, nor slope of ground offered a clue to the direction. Having satisfied myself of all this, there was nothing else to do, so I stretched out on the ground for a night's sleep.

I awoke at dawn. The sun, as usual, rose in the east, so I got my direction at once, and started toward the river, hunting as I went. Within ten minutes, I saw a familiar landmark, and shortly afterwards shot a fat buck weighing a little less than two hundred pounds. He was much darker in color than our white tail deer, and his horns were longer, straighter and more symmetrical. As in all of his species, each horn had one prong projecting forward near its base, and forked into two prongs toward its upper end. By the time Isiong and I had swung him between us on a bamboo pole and gotten him to the boat, we were certain that he was a monster.

CHAPTER XIV

Manila - The Luneta - The Crushed Leg

Vague rumors of a coming polo tournament began to drift down from Manila. Our team had not played since we left San Antonio, and the thought came to us of eager riders spurring for the goal, of spirited ponies dashing, wheeling and racing over the green, of flashing white helmets, the clatter of hoofs and the clear ring of mallets as they struck the ball. It was too much. We had to get into that tournament. Word soon came that the tournament was set for carnival time, and the 9th Infantry team was entered at once. True enough, we had not had a polo stick in our hands for a year, we owned not a pony among us, we had no field to practice on, and the rest of the team was at Iloilo, but in the face of all this we formally entered ourselves for the tournament.

Being thus far committed, we began to look about to see how we were going to put it through. Sight unseen, we arranged to buy some ponies in Manila, and to borrow some others for the tournament, while I picked up a beautiful horse which had just been brought up from Australia. He was a powerful animal, built on the lines of a thoroughbred and with a rich sorrel coat which shone in the sun like burnished copper. Best of all, he had speed. He could run like a race horse - but unfortunately did run exactly that way. When once started, he kept going, and neither skill nor strength seemed to influence him until he made up his own mind that he was ready to stop. In fact, it was this very little trick of his which induced his former owner to part with him.

I started him with a fairly mild bit, and gradually went through everything until I had contrivances in his mouth which would have stopped a railroad train, but still he ran, pulling all the while at the bit like a creature totally devoid of feeling. Then, by a happy chance, I tried the opposite extreme, a soft rubber bit so mild that a colt would scarcely have felt it, and the wild plunging runaway became suddenly gentle as you please, leaving Typhoon's former owner as disgusted as I was delighted.

It is a notorious fact that Filipinos, with the exception of the Pampangans, are almost entirely lacking in any idea of how to handle a horse. The gentlest animal soon begins to kick and bite when left to their care, and their total lack of understanding of, and sympathy for, horses is almost beyond belief. It was, therefore, not until after Narciso had received most careful instructions that he was notified that the spare time which he usually devoted to catching mosquitoes on a tin plate was now to be utilized in grooming and caring for Typhoon. For a week I did everything myself, requiring Narciso to accompany me each time and look on. During the next week, I required him to do the work, while I looked on critically. Time and again Typhoon showed the white of his eye, switched his tail and slightly raised a hind foot as Narciso came within reach; but I carefully schooled the boy in when to pet, when to speak sharply and when to ignore, and all went well. Then with a final word to the effect that the horse would never kick if handled exactly according to my instructions, I turned the job over to Narciso.

Three days later, a pathetic-looking figure came limping into my room. Tears were streaming from his eyes, and his hand was pressed against a semi-circular bruise on his leg. It was Narciso.

"No can do," he whimpered. "Typhoon he kick."

"I told you how to handle that horse," I growled, "and you haven't done it. If you had, he would not have kicked you. I will take away one peso of your pay, and if Typhoon kicks you again, I will take away two pesos. Now, you go back and finish grooming him." So far as I know, he never kicked again.

A week later, our team had reached Manila. The Churchills, who had been at San Antonio with us, had invited all four of us to stay with them at Fort McKinley, several miles out of town, and the hospitality which we enjoyed there is not easily forgotten.

One of the first things we did, was to go in to Manila and drive around the Luneta. We had never done it, and it was the thing to do. To do it properly, it was necessary to get a Victoria, a pretty girl and a bunch of flowers, so we did it properly.

As the sun was setting across the bay and the sky flamed over Mariveles Mountain, the Constabulary band began its concert in the center of the oval green just outside of the massive fortifications of the old walled city. One by one, Victorias, *carruages* and *calesas* rolled up, file in line, and slowly moved around the band stand as the music played. From time to time, a vehicle would turn in to the curb and stop, and its occupants get out and visit from carriage to carriage. It was an old Spanish custom, established years before, and a custom which made the hour of sunset a delightful one to all. You could enjoy the sunset, breathe the fresh sea air, listen to music, see your friends and pay a compliment to a fair one, all at once. What more could you ask?

The Spanish population of Manila was there in force, and among them some of the most distinguished-looking men I have seen in a long while. In fact, an old Spanish gentleman nearly always looks distinguished. With his high forehead, massive brows, clean-cut aquiline nose, piercing eyes and huge mustache, you cannot help feeling that he is a personage. Your mind wanders back to the days of his ancestors, the conquistadores, men who conquered unknown lands and sailed the Spanish Main. And in this hour at the Luneta, Spain still holds sway over Manila. You see here ancient walls with the red tiled roofs peeping over them. You think of galleons bringing gold from far-flung domains, and of adventurous youths, clad in shining armor, seeking new worlds, finding them, conquering them, and laying them at the feet of their king.

What a nation Spain might now be, had the bold spirits who won for her the great empire of her early days taken Spanish women with them to their colonies! But the cold blood of the conquered soon quenched the fire in that of the conqueror, the son of warlike knight was usually a half breed and his grandson scarcely distinguishable from a native. The flower of Spain went out to her colonies, and the blood which should have flowed through generations of the leaders of a great nation was soon lost in the veins of the Indian and Malay. No nation, however great, can long stand such a drain upon the highest product of its race, and it is little wonder that the great Spanish empire could not endure.

Just off the Luneta, were the carnival grounds. Manila was festive, as only a city of light-hearted people can be, and the center of all their celebration was this brightly illuminated area. Within, were displays of hardwoods and Moro brass, quaint weapons inlaid with silver, basketwork, delicate embroideries and mats of fine texture and design, all mixed in with six-legged *carabaos*, merry-go-rounds, human roulette wheels, shoot-the-shoots, and galleries where you could throw a ball and upset a native into a tank of cold water.

Everywhere were natives in masks and fancy costumes, throwing confetti and talking in falsetto voices. Just why a native, who has walked six miles to town and knows no one there, has to talk in a falsetto voice the moment he puts on a mask, I do not know, but invariably he does.

The queen had just been crowned and with all her court, made her way to the masked ball which all of us attended. Another dance pavilion was crowded with soldiers and native dancing girls, nearly all of them Visayans. They were dressed in their gayest colors and most of them danced with a great deal of grace, but they kept you wondering how they managed not to kick off the heelless chinelas into which their bare feet were thrust.

When an appropriate number of hours after bed time had passed, the crowd began wandering home, and we reluctantly followed its example. Very thoughtlessly, I entrusted my neck to the proud possessor of a new automobile, who offered to take me out to McKinley. The car being new, of course we had to talk about it.

"You know," said he, "I believe this about as fast a car as there is in Manila."

I hastily agreed with him in hopes of preventing a demonstration, but he stepped on the accelerator and the car shot forward. Just as he did so, two natives started across the street in front of us. One of them jumped back, just in time to escape, but the other tripped and fell directly in our path.

The brakes screamed, and we swerved to one side, but it was too late. The man tried to roll over, but the heavy wheel caught one of his legs, there was a bump and a horrible crunching sound as his shattered limb was ground into the road.

We rushed back to the unfortunate man, and found him struggling to drag himself to the edge of the road. One leg dangled loosely at an angle to the stump.

Haskell's face was ghastly pale when he saw what he had done.

"To the hospital - quick!" he gasped.

We picked the man up and started for the machine. As we did so, his crushed limb dropped off. It was a wooden leg.

CHAPTER XV

Polo - The Gymkhana - Champagne - The Twelve Apostles

The first day of the polo tournament had come, and mounted on ponies with whom we had scarcely a speaking acquaintance, we pranced out on the beautiful green of Pasay field. I say pranced, and use this word feelingly. Not that we intended to prance, but our ponies did, and that settled it.

We had collected these ponies from various sources and by various means, and every one seemed to have been trained a different way, and that way differed from ours. It has been said that difference of opinion is the basis of horse racing, and this same basis must have had considerable to do with the training of our mounts. In fact, I had heard eloquent dissertations at the club, only the night before, on exactly how a horse should be trained. Two of these I remember. One officer, an excellent horseman, had given us the full benefit of his experiences:

"If you want to do the thing right," he said, "you've got to consider the functions of the various parts of a horse. Everybody knows that a horse is driven forward by his hind legs, and that his front legs are used only to support whim. If his hind legs are south of him, they will drive him north; if they are east of him, they will drive him west. If you want to handle him, then, work on his hind quarters. Use your legs and your spurs on him; bring his feet under him, and he stops; start them going again, and he moves forward. Don't bother about his head, but drive it the way you want it to go, by putting the hind legs in the right place. It's the simple, logical and natural way."

This sounded convincing enough, until another, who was equally successful as a trainer, piped up.

"All of this highbrow stuff about legs is bunk. Wherever a horse's head goes, the rest of the horse has got to follow. When a horse's head starts east, he'll be a mighty peculiar animal if he lets any of the rest of his anatomy go wandering off in any other direction. Control a horse's head, and you control the horse. Leave his hind legs to him. He won't go off and forget them."

These two men had trained the first two ponies which I rode; a third pony never exhibited any indications of having been trained at all. Typhoon alone responded automatically to my aids, and even he had not altogether gotten over some rather original ideas about polo. Johnson, Chaney and Smith were similarly mounted, so we all pranced.

The gong sounded, the white ball rolled in between the two rows of eager players, and the stroke of a mallet sent it bounding down the field, with a mad race of ponies in pursuit. A back stroke from Chaney sent it spinning in the opposite direction, eight ponies swung round, and were off toward the other goal. Johnson was making for the ball, but neck and neck with him was the opposing player. The two ponies were going at top speed, their ears back, their shoulders together, and each pushing with all his strength in an effort to ride the other off of the ball.

Their mounts were evenly matched, neither could gain the advantage, and they rode over the ball. I was following, hard pressed by my opponent, when we both saw the opportunity and started for it. So anxious was I to reach the ball, that for the moment I could not remember for the life of me whether I was riding a stern wheeler, or one which steered from the bow. I tried to turn his head to the northeast, but the boneheaded creature had his rudder on the other end and his head wouldn't turn. By the time I got his hind legs into the southwest, my opponent was gone with the ball.

The game was a wild one, and hard fought on both sides. In the midst of it, a pony went down, its rider threw himself clear, and rolled on the ground just in time to escape the weight of his mount. A second pony jumped over him, but he was on his feet again in a moment. A broken cinch was replaced, and horse and rider were back into the thick of it unhurt.

When the game was over, we looked at the score board.

Whether we had confused our opponents by always doing the wrong and unexpected thing and getting away with it, whether our ponies had played the game for us, or whether we were befriended by pure luck, I do not know, but somehow we had won.

The game over, we went into the club, had a cold plunge in the swimming pool and got into white. The next thing in order was to drink a "shandy gaff." After the violent exertion of a tournament game on a hot day, everyone has to drink something, and at least a quart of it. To fill this need, some genius has concocted the "shandy gaff." It is cool and refreshing, it sparkles and effervesces as tiny bubbles rise to its surface, it quenches the thirst, it is mild enough so that a quart of it is none too much, and yet it has just that delightful quality which creates a restful feeling and happy thoughts. It is the polo drink par excellence. We were sitting in the pergola under a blossoming bougainvillea vine with the soft green of the polo field on one side, and on the other, Manila Bay, with the mirrored reflections of a gorgeous sunset. A native orchestra was playing. Those who had watched the game were sitting at tea tables all about us; we laughed and chatted, and from time to time, we danced.

We did not win the tournament, but we enjoyed it, and after all, that is what it was for. In the semi-finals, we were defeated, and in the final game, we cheered our successful opponents to victory.

When the cups were presented and the last congratulations given, it was decided to have a gymkhana which would include the ladies. Next day, the club was enlivened by dainty figures in smart riding habits, a buzz of conversation, and an amusing program of mounted contests where skill and luck combined to make the outcome uncertain.

There was a bareback race with the riders face backwards for those who didn't mind falling off. Then came tilting, and picking up handkerchiefs while at a gallop. There were races for the ladies, and races in pairs. Men would start at one end of the field, gallop to the other, leading a horse, pin a bouquet on his fair partner, assist her to mount, and race back with her to the starting point. There were contests which included threading needles, putting on Pierrot costumes, carrying eggs in a spoon, and a dozen other features which were as ludicrous as they were enjoyable.

Then came the end of it, the polo banquet. It began at dusk on the *azotea* of the Fort McKinley club. There were cocktails and champagne and jacksnipe on toast, speeches that came from the heart and fell on eager ears, a round of rousing songs, and the warming cheer of good fellowship.

Polo, of all games, carries with it an atmosphere of gentlemanly sportsmanship and happy congeniality which is hard to equal elsewhere. The man who is not a true sportsman has no place in it. Few memories can be happier than those of a tournament on Pasay field - memories of the keen, but chivalrous rivalry of the game; of the dash of ponies over a velvet green; of the meeting with old friends, and the making of new and lasting ones; and last of all its glorious ending in a round of cheer at the banquet.

Conversation had drifted to events at various stations. Someone from Jolo had told of a Moro who had recently run amuck and chopped up two soldiers at the market place before he was shot, and who had been buried with a pig in order that his Mohammedan compatriots might know that his trip to heaven on a white horse for killing Christians had been prevented - an excellent deterrent to others who might have been seeking Heaven in a similar way. There were yarns about the underground river of Palawan, the mouse deer of Cagian Sulu, the terrific eruption of Taal volcano, of hunting the wild and dangerous *tamarao* in Mindoro, of the head-hunters of Bontok, the pygmy Negritos of Zambales, and a dozen other things which linger in my memory.

"You are down at Cebú, aren't you?" said an officer on my left.

"Yes," I replied, "out in the provinces and a long way from

111

the throne."

"Do they still have religious parades at Liluan, just up the coast from you?"

"Yes," I answered, "and I suppose they will continue to have them as long as they can get firecrackers, red-and-white streamers and colored tissue paper."

He smiled reminiscently. "Well, sir," he said, "When I was down there a couple of years ago, they pulled off about the best one I ever saw. They had had most of the saints and sainted one or two at a time, but this Sunday they decided to do the thing right and have nothing less than Jesus and the twelve apostles.

"The padre announced that all properly dressed saints wore flowing white robes; so they got a bunch of night shirts and dolled up these thirteen hombres. Then they cut some tin halos out of the tops of Standard Oil cans, and fastened one of them to the head of every saint with a piece of wire.

"The next thing they did, was to supply each one with some kind of an implement, so that everybody would know that he was a saint. I don't remember what they all had, but St. Andrew had a fish net, St. Matthew had some kind of a pole with a hook on the end of it which was supposed to be a shepherds crook, and St. Peter had the key of heaven. From the size of the key, a sinner of ordinary build might easily have entertained hopes of slipping in through the key hole. A blacksmith in town had made the thing out of an old piece of gas pipe a couple of feet long, with an iron ring welded on to one end of it, and a piece of sheet iron with notches in it on the other.

"They had a time of it. They turned out the band, shot off fire-crackers and the bamboo cannon, marched all over town, and finally ended up at the church, where they had elaborate services in which the apostolic night shirts waved considerably."

"Of course, the padre intended to collect all the costumes after services, but somehow the saintly group slipped through his fingers. Having been a saint all morning, it was too much of a come-down for St. Luke immediately to doff his halo, become an ordinary *tao*, and give up all of his saintly prestige; so he wandered down to the cock fight with the rest following him in a body. Pretty soon they were all perched on the seats of honor along the side of the pit and betting with the rest of the crowd.

"Between fights, they visited a large bowl of tuba in the outside shed, and after half a dozen drinks, became fully confident that they could work miracles. Jesus, having bet on the wrong rooster, was attempting to resurrect his dead chicken, when the judge ran him out of the ring; whereupon his faithful disciple, St. Matthew, stretched out his crook and caught the judge by the leg. Someone reached over and smashed St. Matthew's halo, and then things got generally stirred up. It wasn't long before the apostles were pretty nearly swamped. St. Matthew hooked several of his assailants with his crook, but got tangled up in St. Andrew's fish net and went down. One by one, the saints were martyred - all but St. Peter. With the massive key of heaven, he dented the head of the first man who came near him, and then began systematically laying them out as fast as they got within reach. They threw coconuts at him, tried to rush him, attempted to slip up behind him, but with cracked heads all about him, he was cock of the walk.

"About this time the constabulary arrived and took charge of things; and ten minutes later, a dilapidated group in bent halos and shredded night shirts were marched off to the town jail."

CHAPTER XVI

Elephants - Superfluous Legs - The Walled City - Juan de Ia Cruz – The Leprous Biscuits

I had been shopping on the Escolta, Manila's business street, and hailed a *carromata* to take me to the club. To anyone but a Filipino, the gesture which I gave would have meant "go away," but if you want a native to come to you, you hold your hand up and wave as though you wanted him to get out of your sight at once.

Most of the shops along the Escolta were named. "La Estrella del Norte," "La Esmeralda," "La Fuerta del Sol," and scores of others displayed their signs and invited all to enter and purchase their wares. There were half a dozen Hindu stores, and of all salesmen, these smooth-faced, smiling, white-toothed people surpass any in the world in suave persuasiveness and the ability painlessly to separate you from your cash. I had just come out of one of their shops, and found myself with an empty purse, a large bundle under each arm, and a bowing Hindu giving me a dozen excellent and convincing reasons why I should come back next day - but for the life of me I could not think of what I had in those bundles. All I knew was that they contained some very necessary articles, and that I had gotten them at an astoundingly good bargain.

When I got home that night, it was with intense curiosity that I looked to see what I had bought from the Hindu. The first thing which rolled out of the package was a family of seven ebony elephants, the oldest being six inches high, and the rest tapering down to the baby, who was no bigger than a fat mouse. Seven ebony elephants with ivory tusks! What in the world had ever possessed me to buy them? I am positive that when I got them I had excellent reasons for believing them essential to my happiness, but what those reasons were, I am still trying to remember. Then came a brass candlestick in the shape of a cobra standing on his tail, a pair of Damascene cuff buttons, a red elephant cloth with yellow tassels, a small Satsuma tea pot and a roll of cream-colored pongee silk. - The ways of the Hindu are marvelous.

But to return to the *carromata*. I hailed it, and it stopped; whereas if I had wished to be at all sure of an uninterrupted journey, it would have been far better had I jumped in without permitting it even to slow down.

The driver took up the reins and gave them a shake. "Hooah! Ooey!" - but the horse made no move. Then followed a string of Tagalog epithets in a querulous falsetto voice, beginning with "*lintik*" and punctuated by lashes of the whip, which he swung so as to strike the scrawny little balking pony under the belly - the spot usually selected by *cocheros* for attentions of this sort. As far as the effect of it all was concerned, it only made the animal lay back his ears, hump up his back and give the vehicle a rearward tilt.

I have no idea who invented the *carromata*, but he must have enjoyed riding in rickshaws, and conceived the idea of making an extra-large one and substituting a horse for a coolie. When he got through building it, it evidently struck him that there was no place for the driver, so, as an afterthought he crowded in a tiny improvised seat between the dash board and the knees of the passenger.

A good deal of the tightly-cramped driver's time is spent in wondering what to do with his legs. On several occasions I have seen one-legged carromata drivers; but whether they became drivers because of this convenient lack of anatomy, or whether they whittled themselves down to proper vocational dimensions, I have never been able to ascertain.

Having accomplished nothing so far, the *cochero* dismounted, laid his whip on the ground, and standing directly in front of the horse, caught hold of the two ends of the bit, and by a series of violent jerks, attempted to entice the obdurate beast to start. But jerk as he might, the bewildered animal only gathered his legs under him, threw up his head, cocked his ears forward and squatted slightly behind.

By this time, we had begun to block the traffic in a narrow part of the Escolta. Two heavy carabao carts loaded with bales of hemp moved by with their steady, deliberate pace, ignoring, as usual, all other vehicles, causing a *calesa* containing two painted Japanese girls to back into a large and luxurious-looking automobile, and leaving a liveried chauffeur cursing with a bent in his polished fender.

Meanwhile, a street car came along, and our vehicle had to be gotten out of the way. Our *cochero* enlisted the services of a couple of his compatriots, and after a lengthy conversation in Tagalog, the three got behind the *carromata* and began to push. This seemed to convince the horse that it was less effort to go than to stand still, so he started out at a brisk trot, and the driver hopped in. Anywhere but in Manila, all this would have drawn a crowd, but here it was too common an occurrence to be noticed.

The fact that our horse soon balked again, reminded our driver that his whip was still lying on the ground where he had gotten out, and his desire to return for it led me to change to another vehicle. The new *carromata* took me over the Bridge of Spain, whereupon the *carromata* paused a moment while I looked down on the busy scene in the swift-running Pasig below.

Big *cascos* were tied up against the banks, their cargoes covered with hoods of split bamboo, their bows and sterns painted with puzzling designs in gaudy colors, and nearly all bearing the name of some saint whom its owner desired to flatter. In addition to serving as a lighter, each *casco* provided a home for an amphibious family of Filipinos, who from time to time fished, ate, slept, bailed water out of the *casco* or did nothing at all as occasion required.

Busy, smoke-spouting tugs were puffing, shrieking with their whistle, or heaving at their heavy tows. *Bankas* cut out of single logs and loaded down to their gunwales with freshly-cut hay glided along among the floating tufts of green water-cabbage from the lake above. On shore, long lines of half-naked natives and Chinamen, like swarms of ants, each with his burden, were loading wares on ships bound for the States,

for China, India and for Europe. It was a busy scene.

Our stop on the bridge was only momentary. Soon the long line of vehicles which had delayed us began slowly to move on, and in a moment I was being carried past a well-kept lawn on the approach to the Puerta del Parian. This lawn, surrounding the walled city, occupies the site of the old moat, a dirty, disease-breeding morass, full of decaying vegetation, mosquitoes and twenty-foot pythons.

We passed through the arch of the old gate, and emerged into the walled city. Here I was, rattling along in a rickety *carromata*, over a spot where years before the arrival of the Spaniards, Moros from Borneo had founded the colony of Manila, and were amusing themselves in the praise of Allah and the collection of booty, when in 1571, the Spaniard Legaspi arrived, appropriated their town, and killed their ruler, Rajah Soliman. Three years later, the same little plot of ground had heard the yells of Limahong's Chinese Pirates, as they charged into the Spanish defenses, cut down their leader, Goiti, drove the garrison back toward the Pasig, and were repulsed only by the timely arrival of Salcedo. Perhaps the very stones over which we were bumping had been stained with blood when, Draper, in 1769, took the town with his English fleet, and turned it over to his men to sack and pillage at their will.

Despite the Chinese and Japanese shops, the flock of Filipino children, the lumbering street car and the occasional American policeman, the atmosphere of Spain is still present. Everywhere in the narrow streets, the massive walls, the overhanging second stories, and the red tile roofs were reminders of this once powerful and adventurous nation. Ambition and romance, intrigue and graft, all have had their day in the old walled city. Fair hands have tossed roses through the iron-grated windows in answer to the twanging of the Spanish guitar, plans for conquest and glory have come into being behind those heavy walls; schemes for murder and corruption have been hatched and matured under the same red tiles which are there today. Manila, in the Spanish days, was a long way from Madrid, and loud clamoring within its walls became almost inaudible murmurs by the time they reached Spain. Church and State were working at cross purposes in Europe, and each was seeking to undermine the other's influence in the colonies. With first one and then the other in the ascendancy at home, it is little wonder that the colonial government became confused by garbled reports, and by vague, inconsistent and perplexing policies; and whenever confusion exists in the neighborhood of the treasury, there is always someone who suddenly and mysteriously becomes wealthy.

Beside a little plaza in the walled city stand two buildings. One is the Cathedral, the old seat of ecclesiastical power, and haven of purity and piety of the soul; the other is the Ayuntamiento, the throne of civil administration, and mainstay of the honor and integrity of the former government. While this exponent of purity and piety was sublimely squabbling with the powers of honor and integrity, a delightful little practical joke is said to have been played by a real artist at this form of witticism. A monument to its memory can still be seen in the form of the huge, unfinished foundations of what was to have been an elaborate public building, almost within the shadow of the palace and the church. The story is often told of how this air castle was erected and reported finished by one very successful handler of public funds; and of how his successor, after inveigling the home authorities to send him sufficient funds to repair the roof, which he assured them had caved in as the result of an earthquake, carefully cleared his accounts by reporting the building destroyed by fire.

Whether resulting from further competition between Church and State or otherwise, there rapidly grew up in the Philippines two large and widely distributed mestizo families. Aside from the legitimate children of Spaniards who had married native women, the governing race had numerous offspring of a more or less unofficial nature. It was far from the thoughts of their native mothers to rob these children of the prestige to be gained by a family name indicative of their Spanish parentage; and it was perhaps equally far from the minds of their Spanish fathers to bestow their own names upon their haphazard children. The soldiers came in for a considerable share in this offhand parentage; and whenever the immediate progenitor of a child was indeterminate, but unquestionably military, the child was usually christened "Del Rey" - "Of the King." But in nothing was the Church to be outdone; and the Padre often became very much of an ancestor among his flock, with the result that the family of "De la Crus" - "Of the Cross" rivals, and perhaps even outnumbers that of Del Rey.

But however much we may condemn the laxity and corruption among the old Spanish priesthood, we cannot fail to remember that there were among them, men of real piety, who toiled, suffered untold hardships and gave their lives that Christianity might be carried to the people of remote corners of the earth. Not content with stopping in the Philippines, they pressed on to Japan, where torture and almost certain death awaited them. The Emperor of Japan, despairing of stopping them any other way, resorted to a counter-move. When missionaries were sent to Japan, he straightaway rounded up lepers and sent them to the Philippines. One hundred and fifty of these were landed in Manila at one time, where the priests, instead of killing them, as had been expected, established the hospital of San Lazaro, where these unfortunate people were cared for.

Leprosy, that dread disease of the Orient, is by no means rare in the Philippines; but as fast as cases are discovered, they are sent to the leper colony at Culyon, on Palawan. Here, they have always been well cared for, but for a long time they kept escaping, and going to other islands to spread the disease. A reward was offered to the neighboring Moros for the return of escaped lepers, but still they escaped. Then some genius added a further reward for the return of the body of a leper, who might be killed while attempting to elude capture. The Moros were not slow to perceive that the reward offered for a leper killed while escaping exceeded, by few pesos that paid for a live one. This fact also impressed itself upon the inmates of the leper colony, when they observed that no live ones were ever brought back. Since then, there has been little trouble with attempts to escape.

In Cebú, I once visited the Lazareta with a doctor, who had asked me to assist him in making photographs for his use in the study of leprosy. Nearly two hundred lepers, in all stages of the disease, had just been collected there in the annual round-up for shipment to Culyon. It was a horrible sight to see men, women, and even children, literally falling to pieces. Many were covered with ghastly-looking spots and nodules, others had terribly distorted features, and gaping holes where their noses had been. The fingers and toes of a large number had already withered and dropped off. Their hands and feet would go next, then their arms and legs, if death did not mercifully claim them sooner.

With all its frightful symptoms, leprosy is nevertheless said to be painless, and it was a strange and incongruous sight to see its victims laughing, singing, and apparently enjoying themselves. It was only those who had just been taken with the disease whose faces bore an expression of inconsolable sadness.

Among the latter was a girl, neatly dressed and in the full bloom of her youth. She had no visible signs of the disease, and held herself aloof from the rest. While I was arranging the camera, she came up to speak to me. A touch of Spanish blood had given regularity to her features, and her dark expressive eyes were full of tears.

"I am not like those," she said, "and I don't want to go to Culyon."

I tried to console her by saying that there were many like her at Culyon, that it was only by going there that she could hope to receive the medical attention of experts, and that the doctors were well on their way toward discovering a cure.

"But I don't want to leave my old man," she protested. "The constabulary took me this morning, and they won't let me see him again."

"Who is your old man?" I asked.

"He is a soldier. He is cook of F Company at the *cuartel*."

Her reply filled me with horror. F Company! My own company!

"How long have you been living with him since you got leprosy?"

"Only six months," she replied. "I couldn't tell him, because then he would have left me. Will they send him to me at Culyon?"

I lost no time in getting back to the cuartel where I dropped in at the hospital to notify the regimental surgeon about the cook.

"He is already here," said the doctor, "and has lost about ten pounds since he heard about his *querida*, Florencia. Moreover everybody in F Company is scared to death at the thought of having eaten leprous biscuits for the past six months. I have examined at least fifty mosquito bites since noon on soldiers in that company who felt certain that they had the first symptoms of leprosy."

"And how about the cook; is there any hope for him?"

"Yes, he seems to be all right so far. It's a peculiar disease. Sometimes people seem to catch it very easily, and at other times they live in intimate association with lepers for years, and never get it. In a few cases, perfectly good children have even been born of leprous parents. It's a disease we don't know much about."

Happily for the cook, he escaped, but he ate, drank, and bathed in disinfectants for a year; and as for F Company, it was a long time before their appetites were good.

CHAPTER XVII

In Old Fort Santiago - Legs and Wings - Jose Rizal
Coleoptera - The Infant and the Beer Bottle

Long after the polo tournament was over, I was again in Manila on temporary duty, living at Fort Santiago, that picturesque corner of the walled city built by the Spaniards to protect the mouth of the Pasig River. From the second story of my house, I could walk out onto the top of the old wall, which was broad enough to furnish a tennis court and a pretty little palm garden where we sat in the evening and watched the bay.

I shared the house with a young officer on duty at the Manila ordnance depot, who, in addition to being a delightful companion, something of a linguist and a very accomplished musician, had the further distinction of being a "native son." Needless to say, I soon received full confirmation of various rumors which I had heard to the effect that they grew bigger ones in California; that the fruits, flowers and bathing girls of this great State surpassed all others in the world; that it was the fire and not the earthquake that damaged San Francisco; and that certain cold, drizzly periods which had been experienced along the Pacific coast were "very exceptional weather."

Together we kept open house, and scarcely an evening passed that we did not pick up a group of friends on the Luneta or at the club and bring them home for dinner. No matter how many dropped in, our Chinese cook was always equal to the occasion. One evening he had to stretch six snipe so as to serve them to seven people and we wondered how he was going to do it. To my surprise, when the snipe came in, there were seven of them. I was still wondering how in the world he had gotten the other one, when I started to eat my own bird, and found it to have a most peculiar anatomy. The rascal had taken a piece of mutton and cut it into the exact shape of a snipe's body. Then he had removed a neck from one of the birds, a leg from another, and wings from others and attached these to the mutton body in such a way as to make a highly creditable composite bird, entirely suitable for the host. While I was eating it, I saw John's eye peering through the crack of the door. For me to have betrayed him to our guests would have broken his heart.

John had very peculiar ideas about turkeys. One day I told him to get one of these birds from the market, and later saw it tied by the leg to the back steps. All of its blood seemed to have gone to its head, which was of a brilliant red color, one of its wings was hanging down, and it was blinking in a blear-eyed sort of a way. When I approached, the turkey tried to move, but fell down and began to flounder around in an attempt to get up again.

"John," I said, "that turkey is sick. You take him back and get another one."

"No sicky," he assured me. "He ol-light."

"What in the world have you been doing to him?"

"Givvim lum," he answered.

"What did you give him rum for?"

"Makum tender," said John.

John's real masterpiece was his "lice an' cully." He would make a pyramid of flaky, snow-white rice, and cover it with the most deliciously spiced of curry sauces. Then he would send in a dish divided into over a dozen compartments, each filled with a different condiment. One contained chutney, another ginger pickle and others toasted coconut, chow-chow, the yolks of boiled eggs spiced and chopped fine, grated onions crisped and browned and many more which only John could name, and which blended together into the seasoning of a dish fit for the gods.

The rainy season was on; vines and shrubs were covered with blossoms, the fire trees blazed with their brilliant masses of bloom, and every plant showed the exquisite freshness of rapid and luxuriant growth. A vine on the side of our house grew an inch every three hours; and I measured the pencil-like shoot at the top of a large banana plant and found that it had grown two feet in twenty-four hours, after which it unrolled into a broad leaf.

One pleasant feature of the rainy season was that we had plenty of sunshine. It rained every day, but the rains usually came in short violent downpours at fairly regular hours, and the rest of the time it was clear. During a large part of the season in Manila, it poured down every night while we were at dinner, and then almost invariably cleared off in time for us to sit out on the *azotea* when we got up from the table.

One evening we were having the usual thunderstorm while a couple of officers from Corregidor were in at dinner with us. As one of them looked out through the broad window, a vivid flash of lightning made everything visible outside.

"Hello!" he said. "There's the old convent across the way that Jose Rizal spoke about in his Nolle me Tangere. Do you remember his story of the flash of lightning, and the drenched figure of a nun up there on the roof, and of her wails and shrieks over the horrible fate which was being forced upon her by the friar? He certainly drew a rough picture of some of those old friars."

A TOUCH OF OLD SPAIN

"I'm inclined to think that there's a good deal of bunk about Rizal's being such a great Filipino," replied our other guest, "and don't see why they make such a fuss over him. To begin with, he was a *mestizo*, and when he tried to make his heroine attractive, he laid stress upon the fact that she was almost white. Of course, he may have done this to flatter his rather pale mistress, whom he married by way of respectability in his cell the night before he was executed. His book probably gave a good picture of the corruption among the friars in those days, but that hardly entitles him to being made so much of."

"I really believe," he continued, "that there is a good deal in the story that the Americans are altogether responsible for his being considered a hero. You see, when we first came over here, the natives didn't have anyone of their own race who had ever done anything particularly conspicuous, and the chances were that sooner or later they would start by naming streets after some prominent *insurrecto* against us, and wind up by putting his statue in the plaza and considering him a great man. Consequently, to keep them from making a hero out of someone who opposed us, we made much of an *insurrecto* against Spain, and everybody was perfectly satisfied."

"You could hardly call him an insurrecto," replied the other, "because he never actually opposed Spanish sovereignty. What he was really after was the expulsion of the friars from the Philippines. He had a European education and considerable skill as a doctor, and could just as well have left the Philippines and lived comfortably elsewhere; but he had the nerve to stay and fight the most powerful and unscrupulous organization in the islands, and he wound up by being shot for trying to help his people. He opposed the friars, and the friars killed him; and it's very doubtful if they didn't stretch their evidence considerably when he was tried and condemned. It hardly seems probable that he would have had a lot of seditious papers in his trunk at the very time when he was pretty certain that his baggage was going to be examined. Whether a man has much ability or not, when he has the nerve to tackle an organization like the friars of Rizal's day, and when he can meet his death with the calm dignity which Rizal showed before the firing squad, I'm perfectly willing to hear people call him a hero,"

Before the evening was over, we had arranged a hunt at Mariveles for the following Sunday. None of us had ever been there, so we included in our party a young civilian named Zimmer from the Department of Agriculture, who was familiar with the lay of the land, and who, among other things, was a naturalist and collector of "specimens." He had already gotten together a marvelous collection of the most beautiful birds in the islands, he could produce almost any kind of a reptile from certain elaborate tin boxes in his house, and when it came to the parilia and coleoptera he had them by the thousand.

He told us that Mariveles was an interesting place to hunt, and from the paraphernalia he brought along, he must have thought so. To begin with, he was armed with a large, heavy, double-barreled shot gun with an auxiliary chamber in one barrel, and a .45 caliber revolver which he said might come in handy if his shot gun happened to be loaded with bird shot when a pig or deer came along. Hanging around his neck was a pair of field glasses ready for instant use; and a large leather pouch suspended from a strap across one shoulder contained a bird skinning outfit, absorbent cotton, a bottle of arsenic, some paper tags, a folding net, and various peculiar-looking jars and tin boxes. A camera dangled from his other shoulder, and a belt around his waist held the sheath of a hunting knife, and cartridges of various sizes and shapes.

We had scarcely gotten started on our hunt when a large wild chicken flew up in front of us, and before anyone else could get into action, there was a rattling of jars and tin cans, a roar from Zimmer's gun and the cock came tumbling down. Zimmer started up a steep bank to get it, when his foot slipped and he and his whole outfit were spread out all over the ground. As he did not get up at once, I went over to see if he had accidentally swallowed some of his arsenic, but found that in spite of a tear across the knee of his trousers, and a couple of scratches on one cheek, he was wreathed in smiles of satisfaction.

"My! That was lucky," he said. "If I hadn't fallen down, just look what I would have missed." He pointed to a small speck which was slowly crawling across the surface of a stone.

"Do you know what that is?" he asked.

As far as I was concerned, it was only another bug, and I said so.

"The Smithsonian," he continued, "has been trying to get a specimen of the female of that species of beetle for the past four years, and here it is."

He picked up the beetle with a pair of forceps, and dropped it on a piece of blotting paper in the bottom of one of his jars, where it gave a couple of kicks and died of the fumes rising from the paper.

His next find was a "flying dragon," a yellow-and-black lizard about six inches long with a sort of keel on the lower side of his neck and ribs which extended some distance beyond his body and were connected by a web like a bat's wing. With these wings, he could sail from tree to tree much after the fashion of a flying squirrel. We got a few more chickens and some pigeons, and were starting back, when we jumped a doe which disappeared without being fired at. I went over to where she had gotten up, and found a fawn not over a couple of days old and scarcely able to toddle along. It showed no fear of me whatever, but stood looking with large, brown eyes as I approached. I picked him up in my arms and carried him a couple of miles to the *banka* which took us to Corregidor, where we met the boat for Manila. All the time I was carrying him, the fawn seemed entirely unperturbed, and finally, in hopes of satisfying his hunger, looked me over very carefully and took one of my ears in his mouth.

It was not entirely without embarrassment that I went into the English drug store the next day to make a purchase. A tall, grave-looking Britisher was standing behind the counter measuring powders into small capsules and putting these into a box.

I would like a---a----baby nipple," I said, with the diffidence which any bachelor might have felt upon a like occasion. "A good strong one," I added, as he produced a large assortment.

"For a youngster about how old?" he inquired with a professional air.

"About three days," I replied.

"Then you want something very soft and smooth," he advised, "with small perforations."

"No," I insisted, "I need one that will stand a lot of chewing, and I want the largest perforations you have, so that I can get the milk down him in a hurry."

The Englishman looked a little puzzled, but pulled out a bottle like a small fruit jar with a rubber contraption pulled over the top. "This," he assured me, "is a bit better than the ordinary kind. The large neck makes it easy to sterilize, and entirely sanitary."

"No," I said, "I don't need that; I can use an old beer bottle, and never expect to sterilize it anyway."

As I left the store, I looked back, to see this serious-minded Englishman, leaning over his capsules and shaking his head in grave and sober meditation.

CHAPTER XVIII

The One That Got Away - Why They Wouldn't Sink
The Smell of Bamboo Smoke - The Bats of Montelban
Week-ends Around Manila - The Spirit of the Waterfall.

For some days, Birkett, an Englishman living in Manila, had been urging me to go fishing with him in the bay. As a matter of fact, it took very little urging, and I went at my first opportunity. In the early afternoon, we got a little boat, and were towed to a reef near the naval station of Cavite, where we let out our lines and began to fish. We had stout rods with reels about the size of alarm clocks, each holding three hundred yards of heavy tarpon line, and before the evening was over, we found that even this was none too strong. For a while, we baited with minnows and shrimp and caught a couple of three-foot Philippine pompano and several smaller fish, after which we switched to a lure of white feathers and began to troll.

It looked like a good evening, for the bay was dotted with square- sailed Japanese fishing boats and, judging from the amount of activity on their decks, they were having luck.

Soon Birkett's rod was bent double, and his line began to go out at a lively rate. I drew in my own tackle and handled the boat, while he worked the drag of his reel against the frantic rushes of his fish. Time and again he pumped and reeled it within thirty or forty yards, only to see his line tear out for a hundred more yards and have the work all to do over again.

Birkett, with the skill of an old fisherman, always kept a taut line, took advantage of every chance to reel in, and foiled every attempt which the fish made to free itself of the hook. The rushes gradually became fewer and shorter; then they ceased altogether; and at last a huge alligator-like mouth gaped near the boat, where a gaff soon landed his beautiful five-foot barracuda.

We each followed with a large horse mackerel, and were on the point of starting home, when my reel let out a shriek, and my rod was almost jerked into the water. Out went the line, one hundred yards, two hundred yards, but still no sign of checking or turning. I thumbed my reel as much as I dared without danger of breaking the line, but still the creature tore away.

Meanwhile, Birkett had swung the boat round, and was following in order to ease the strain, but do what we might, three hundred yards of a line which would have held the largest tarpon was carried out and snapped off like a thread. Birkett told me that he had similar experiences, and that from their actions, he believed the fish to have been large barracuda in every case. Someday I hope to catch one and know.

On our return, we went over to the English club, where most of Birkett's British friends were having their abominable drink of tepid Scotch and soda before dinner. Why they take this drink in a lukewarm state and consistently refuse to put ice into it, no American can understand. And yet they drink it, great quantities of it, and insist that it is healthy.

There is perhaps nothing that will make a man go to pieces more quickly in the tropics than excessive drinking; but the amount of drinking which constitutes excess on the part of any individual is very largely dependent upon the amount of exercise he takes. The Englishman drinks his Scotch and soda, or perhaps his seven Scotch and sodas, as regularly as the day comes around; but along with it, he always has his polo, his three sets of tennis, his swim or his ride. He is regular and methodical in his work, his play, his rest and even his dissipation, and nearly always you will find him fit.

There are many theories about living in the tropics, theories about actinic rays requiring spine pads and orange-colored underclothing, theories of the evils resulting from cold baths, the necessity for flannel bandages about the abdomen, and dozens of others; but I have seen very few obsessed with these theories who were not cherishing some pet ailment at the same time.

We were sitting at a table cut from a single plank of red nara, talking over the afternoon's sport, and gradually increasing the size of the fish which had gotten away. Birkett had been in Manila ever since the Spanish regime, and somehow our talk drifted around to the early days of American occupation.

"Corking sort of fellow, old Dewey," said Birkett, filling his glass. "I was here, you know, when he came.

"In the afternoon, one of the blooming gunboats that the Spanish had came puffing into the bay, and the blarsted thing never stopped until it was clean up the Pasig river; so we thought the American boats would be coming in a bit and that it would be rather interesting. We sat up all night at the club playing poker and waiting for them and in the morning, by Jove, they did come.

"They steamed right over to the Luneta, where the Spaniards had a little gun; in fact, they had two little guns. When they saw the Americans they loaded up one of them and took a shot at the fleet, and, by Jove, the fleet took a shot back at them. The funny thing about it was, that one of the Englishman that had been with us was in a *calesa* on his way home for breakfast, while the rest of us were still having our Scotch and soda; and, you know, the shot went clean over the little gun, and right over the calesa, too. And so the Englishman turned around, and drove his calesa all the way back to the club, and had a bit more Scotch and soda.

"Having captured the Luneta with this shot, the American fleet went over to where the Spanish boats were, and began firing at them; but the blarsted things wouldn't sink, and they couldn't understand it; so they went over to the other side of the bay for a while - I suppose to get a cocktail, I can't think what else they would have gone for.

"After they had talked it over a bit, they came back and fired some more, and, by Jove, the bally things still wouldn't sink. They couldn't, you see because they were already resting on the bottom. The Spaniards had scuttled them. The Spanish comandante had taken all the money for ammunition, and used it for himself.

"Really, it was all very ripping, for the American admiral was a jolly good sort of a chap. We met him afterwards."

We chatted on, and perhaps the hours were small when we stopped, for there is a deal to talk about in Manila. The old town, with all its gaiety, its many races, its quaint customs and odd corners, presents a varied and unending store of delight to anyone who will explore its resources.

You can drop in any time at Clarke's, or "Clarky's" as the natives call it, for a noonday luncheon, and hear seven or eight different languages being spoken at tables around you. You can wander down Pipin Street and find yourself in a bit of China, with all the signs in Chinese characters, pig-tailed coolies all around you, and scrupulously neat women toddling about in blue and purple

131

pajamas. You can happen out near the Laloma church at the proper time, and find *flaggalantes* flogging themselves and their friends into insensibility, and rubbing dirt into their wounds in the fervent fanaticism of their penance. You can walk down the Escolta and pass Europeans, turbaned Hindus, Japs, Syrian tradesmen, Chinamen, Anamite sailors from the rice and carabao boats, and natives of half a score of tribes, all within a block. You can go in five minutes from palatial Spanish residences to nipa shacks on stilts. And always you can inhale the faint aroma of burning bamboo, that fragrant incense of the East, which sets the mind at rest, and fills it with happy thoughts.

Week-ends near Manila need never be uneventful. My first took me to Montelban, where a number of us ate picnic suppers at the foot of a mountain gorge, in an atmosphere intoxicating with the perfume of the *ilang-ilang*. Just at dark, what appeared to be a column of smoke began to pour from a cave on the mountainside. It rose, swirled about, spread in every direction, and then broke up and melted away into the darkness.

"What in the world is that?" I asked an old timer.

"A swarm of bats," he told me. "They roost up there in a large cave during the day, and every evening about this time they all come out together to make a night of it."

Like everyone else in Mann, I took one trip to see the bamboo organ at Las Piñas and visited the Virgin of Antipolo. This image is credited with performing all sorts of miraculous deeds, and in gratitude for her beneficial acts, she has been presented with great numbers of jeweled gifts. She is said to have restored health to invalids, to have allowed cripples to throw away their crutches and walk, to have returned lost property and hundreds of other things. Among her most noteworthy deeds, was stopping a storm that threatened to swamp the ship which was conveying her over from Mexico; but why she ever permitted the storm to start, and allowed it run its usual course before she stopped it, no one has ever attempted to explain.

Another week-end found me in the crater of Taal, that treacherous volcano in the center of a deep lake, which, after slumbering peacefully for over half a century, went off in the night with a bang and killed about twelve hundred people. In the bottom of the crater is another lake, and when I got to it, I was so warm from the climb that I decided to take a swim in its volcanic waters. Far from being refreshed, however, I found the water tepid, almost as buoyant as Great Salt Lake, and so strong with minerals that it made my skin tingle and my eyes smart with pain.

Trip after trip I made, and for beauty of scenery, I enjoyed nothing so much as a day in the cañon of Pagsanjan, where in a canoe, I followed a rushing stream which wound between vertical cliffs of rock, broken here and there by waterfalls, and draped with hanging vines, air plants and blossoming orchids. Kingfishers with iridescent plumage flew up and dove the cañon, diving occasionally for minnows, and as I approached the mouth of the narrow gorge, a large troupe of monkeys chattered, made faces and shook branches at me as I passed. With two boys poling, pushing and dragging the canoe, I reached the upper falls which spurted from the rocks into a deep basin below.

Going up had been a laborious process, but coming down was full of thrills. One boy stood up in the bow with a pole, and the other steered from behind with a paddle, as the little dug-out shot through swirling rapids of white water which roared and covered us with spray. In the midst of one of these, I saw the boy in the bow plant his pole in a frantic sort of a way, and then rise in the air like an insane pole-vaulter. Simultaneously, the canoe gave a violent lurch, rose half way out of the water, spun round and turned over.

I landed among the minnows, and although the water was shallow, the current swept me off my feet at once, and I found myself skidding along the bottom in a sitting position, completely submerged except for one hand, which protruded like a periscope and held my camera. At the foot of the rapids, I emerged, hatless and spluttering, collected boat, boys and paddle, and proceeded without further mishap.

Another scene which shall always linger in my memory is the falls near Los Baños known as the Upper Falls of Pasagnan. After following a wooded ravine where tree-ferns grew twenty feet high, I came upon a cliff whose dripping rocks were half-clothed in moss and hanging vines. Over the cliff, a mountain stream plunged in a white column of mist-shrouded spray, and fell into a shaded pool among giant trees below. There was nothing of the thunder and awe-inspiring grandeur of a Niagara, but the cool, refreshing sound of many fountains, the fragrance of dewy leaves and wild flowers, a loveliness and mystery combined. As I scrambled over the rocks below the falls, I caught sight of the figure of a man, robed in white, standing on a stone in the edge of the pool.

His arms were extended, his eyes lifted toward the falling water, and his lips murmuring in prayer. He was a Japanese priest, who had come from Heaven knows where to stand in this lovely spot and commune with the Spirit whose presence seemed to hang like an enchantment in the shifting mist of the waterfall. The spell of some unseen hand held me back, forbidding me to intrude upon his devotions. For a moment, I watched him from a distance; then, silently, I slipped away, leaving him in fervent prayer to that God of Nature that dwells in all things beautiful.

CHAPTER XIX

Pygmies - The Spear Trap - Seeing America - On with the Dance – Smoking Backwards – Dame Fashion and the Gee-string

A long, sultry day of firing machine guns on the range at Camp Stotsenburg had been hot and tiring, and the contrast of a breezy porch, white uniforms and tea at sunset was particularly refreshing. A boy brought out a tray, lighted an alcohol lamp, glided into the house and reappeared with no sound except the tinkle of ice in frosted silver goblets. He was followed by our hostess, a Virginian of rare accomplishments, who never entrusted the filling of those goblets to any but her own fair hands.

Below us, beyond the even green of the parade ground, was the Pampangan plain, fertile and well cultivated, with the rugged peak of Aryat sticking up out of the middle of it in grim protest against the monotonous flatness of the country at its feet. On the other side of us were mountains, piled higher and higher, until Pinatubo, towering above the rest, played hide and seek with us among the cloud-masses which hung about its summit.

You cannot look at Pinatubo without wanting to climb it, yet I have never heard of a white man who has stood on its highest point. Miles of dense tropical jungle surround it, and little bands of pygmy Negritos wander among its foothills, sleep wherever night overtakes them, and live on the deer, wild boar and monkeys that fall victim to their arrows. You may run across one of these bands, but more often they will melt away like shadows at your approach and watch your movements unseen from the forest shadows. If you talk to one of these little men, he will tell you weird tales of the mountains, of strange creatures that are some-times seen on its slopes, of spirits that rise out of its caves and walk in the mist. He will tell you, too, of a place where gold can be piled up in lumps from the ground - but he will not show you the place, the spirits forbid. And if you want to climb the moun-tain, he will shake his kinky little head, and leave you wondering what thoughts are going on inside of it.

As we chatted on the verandah, a dark-looking object about the size of a twelve-year-old boy came shambling down the side-walk and stopped in front of the house. An old-style artillery officer's full-dress cap, about seven sizes too large for him, was balanced on his shock of kinky, black hair, an old blue coat with brass buttons which would have held two of his size was buttoned up to his chin, and his naked, black legs seemed to hang down from under the coat, rather than support him. It was Lucas, chief of a small group of Negritos who had come down from the hills, and taken up their abode in grass lean-tos near the post. After looking us over for half a minute, he climbed the stairs, placed a large flowering orchid plant on the porch and asked for some tobacco.

Having gotten this, he still hung around as though he had something on his mind, and finally disclosed the fact that he was having family troubles, and had come for advice. He had gotten a new wife, the others being old, and she had run away. He had brought her back, beaten her and tied her to a tree, but during the night she had gotten away and stolen his favorite son, and sent word that if he came after her again she would kill the child. Now his other women were laughing at him and calling him an old man. How did the Americans keep their wives? What should he do?

You can imagine the large clusters of advice which he received, and the dire things which might have happened to him had he tried to follow any of it. He started off, confused and disheartened, when our hostess tripped down the steps after him, whispered something into his ear, and sent him off looking amused and hopeful. What she told him, I have never been able to persuade either her or Lucas to divulge, but three days later, the strayed wife was back and Lucas had presented his fair advisor with a dozen orchid plants in token of his gratitude.

At Stotsenburg, l could find out very little about the Negritos. The presence of these primitive aborigines of the islands somewhere back in the jungle was taken for granted and aroused little interest or comment. Aside from Lucas and his handful of satellites, none of them came near the post, and no one in the garrison seemed disposed to explore their haunts. To anyone not living at Stotsenburg, this apathy was difficult to understand; but it was the old story of the man living within a stone's throw of one of the wonders of the world and dying without seeing it.

When the machine gun practice was over, we had about four days to spend at Stotsenburg before returning to our respective stations, and it was an easy matter to get up a party of two more visiting officers who had enough curiosity to agree to a trip among the Negritos. We decided to start in the early morning, carrying only enough plunder to enable us to be respectable among savages, and maintain our prestige by having someone else do the carrying. We engaged two Pampangan *cargadores*, directed Lucas to provide two more of his own race, and got my own Pampangan boy, Andres Maneloto, as interpreter. Beside these, we were, of course, to take Lucas, who would get us in touch with the Negritos and act in the capacity of guide, mascot, and general source of amusement.

At sunrise we assembled for the start. Lucas, who evidently regarded his own mission as one of diplomatic importance, appeared properly attired for occasions of ceremony. On his head was an old khaki cap decorated with a pink feather; he was robed in a cream-colored pajama coat minus one sleeve, and carried a sort of scepter fashioned from a mop handle with the aluminum top of a catsup bottle screwed on to one end of it. From beneath all this finery, his naked black legs proudly protruded.

Everything being ready, our little group crossed the open cogon-grass ridge just east of the post, and started for the Banban River. When we reached this stream, we were hot and thirsty, and its cool, clear water, running swiftly down from shaded canons above was more than inviting. Our natives, immune to the amoebic dysentery which lurks in nearly all Philippine waters, stuck their bills in the stream and pumped themselves full, but the rest of us had to content ourselves with the boiled contents of our canteens. For the white man in the tropics, boiled water is the only safe thing.

After a ten-minute rest for the cargadores, we forded the Banban and started wading up the bed of one of its tributaries. Up this little stream, we splashed for some seven or eight miles, following the tunnel which it made through the otherwise impenetrable tangle of vegetation. Great tree ferns, ten to twenty feet high, grew tall and rank in the damp, steam-like atmosphere; vines and branches interlaced above us, and even the noonday tropical sun was subdued to a twilight by the leafy bowers overhead.

Giant trees towered around us, some with flattened buttresses projecting at their bases, some with strange-looking roots hanging down from every limb and groping for the ground, some with gnarled and twisted trunks, weird, misshapen and fantastic; soft, fleshy leaves adorned others while many had masses of fruit or berries hanging in clusters from their trunks near the ground.

Most peculiar of all was the strangling fig. The seed of this often takes root in the upper fork of another tree. Here it lives as a parasite, eventually sending down numerous roots to choke and strangle the tree which gave it support. In several cases, we saw where the original tree had died and completely rotted away, leaving its twisted slayer standing like a grim skeleton of Death above the remains of its victim.

Orchids, and parasitic plants grew in the forks of trees or projected from the bark of their trunks. On every side were the glossy leaves of the banana and the palm, and above the thorny masses at their bases, clumps of bamboo rose in graceful plumes.

My boy Andres pointed out a variety of bamboo slightly slenderer than the rest and said, "Good water." I looked rather dubious, and he walked over, snipped off a joint of it with his bolo, and handed it to me. It was a third full of delicious cool water.

Shortly after noon, we came to a large table-like rock projecting from the bank and affording an excellent place to rest and cook dinner. Lucas was walking slightly in the lead, and by a ridiculous pantomime, called our attention to the propriety of halting for "chow". He stopped, placed both hands on his stomach and assumed a most hollow, woebegone expression. Then, looking tenderly at the bag of rice on the head of one of the Negritos, he began to lick his chops and take on an imploring attitude. Such an appeal could not be resisted, so we made ready for our noon-day meal. Andres looked after our own needs, and one of the Negritos, under the direction of Lucas, prepared rice for the boys.

Were you to say to the average white man, "Here is some raw rice. I have no pot for you, but go ahead and boil it for your dinner," the likelihood of his going hungry that day would be very strong. But not so with the Negrito. Instead of asking for a cooking utensil, one of our heathens borrowed my bolo and cut a couple of green bamboo joints about eight inches in diameter for kettles. In the side of each, he made a small opening, and through these filled the joints a third full of rice. He then filled the remaining space with water, stuck in some leaves for flavoring, closed the openings with chips, and put the joints on the fire. Twenty minutes later, he took them off, fairly bursting from the steam which hissed from their openings.

A couple of whacks with the bolo, and two large cylinders of steaming rice were dumped from the split joints onto a banana leaf, a can of sardines, oil and all, was poured on top of the pile, and a circle of boys squatting around this delicacy, began to eat with the noises usually made by a mammal at its first feedings. Judging from the uniformity of their table manual, it must have been governed by some form of bamboo etiquette. Each ate with one hand picking up as much rice as he could hold between his thumb and fingers without getting any on his palm. He then leaned forward, rolled his eyes upward, stuck his thumb into his mouth, and deftly slid the whole gob after it with his fingers. The thing was done with a dexterity only possible after long and enthusiastic practice.

A mile or so up the stream, the Negrito in lead parted some branches and led us off into a tunnel-like trail, so low in places that we had to lean over to avoid the vines and *bejuco* overhead. The trail was full of wild boar tracks, and was evidently used by these animals to go to water.

The Negrito pointed to a split stake at one side of the trail having a flat piece of bamboo stuck into the cleft making a cross. "Bugsuk," he said. This meant nothing to any of us, so we continued without paying any attention to it until we noticed that the Negrito in front began to walk with the utmost caution, examining every inch of the trail minutely as though he expected it to be strewn with tacks.

Fifty yards beyond the split stake, he held up his hand for us to stop, pointed to one side of the path and repeated the word "*bugsuk*." The tip of a wicked-looking spear-head just protruded from the bushes and pointed across be trail. Attached to the spear, was a powerful bamboo spring, bent back and held by means of a trigger in such a way that anything touching an innocent-looking vine across the trail would release the spring and be transfixed by the spear. From the looks of the thing, it had already done its work on more than one unfortunate animal. Fifty yards beyond, we found another split stake indicating the presence of the trap.

Our trail led us out of the woods to the foot of a grass-covered ridge up which we struggled. Seven-foot grass, stiff, tough and with edges like razors, a sun that fairly burned into our flesh, an atmosphere like stifling steam, and a long steep hill to climb proved no easy combination. When finally we staggered to the top, reached the cool breeze and the short grass, with one accord, we dropped on the ground for a long rest.

Stretching away below us, until earth and sky blended in a distant blur, was a vast plain, dotted with villages, checkered and mottled with plantations of rice and cane. To see so much of the world at one time, was too much for the Pampangan cargadores. They had spent their narrow lives in the low country, and fear of Negrito arrows had always kept them far from the hills. They looked and marveled.

"Which way is America?" asked one.

I pointed to the east. He borrowed my field glasses, and began to sweep the horizon.

"What are you looking for?" I inquired.

"San Francisco," he replied.

After crossing the ridge, we again struck into the dark forest, following the trails made by the deer and pigs that abounded there. Bamboo crosses and spear traps became more numerous, so we felt sure that we were getting into the Negrito country. Also, to be certain that our guide played no jokes on us by stepping over vines, we had one of his compatriots and a Pampangan cargadore follow immediately behind him.

Eventually we encountered a Negrito, who started to run, but Lucas called him back and he joined us. After a talk with Lucas, our new companion assumed the duties of guide, and led us to the edge of a deep cañon with a stream at the bottom of it. Here, as well as we could make out, the domains of Lucas ended; and certain formalities would have to be gone through with before our expedition could venture farther without being considered hostile. None of us had any idea of being hostile, so in spite of our desire to push on, we agreed on having the formalities.

Accordingly, Lucas and our guide walked out on a spur overlooking the cañon, and began a series of unearthly yells. Soon they were answered by equally discordant sounds from a tiny black figure, whose kinky head bobbed up out of the tall grass on the opposite hill. Then three men descended into the ravine from the other side, and one of our Negritos met them at the bottom. Through our field glasses, we could see an excited pow-wow, and at length the four came up and joined us.

After giving assurance that we were on a peaceful mission, and had no intention of shooting anyone, we learned that a great feast was taking place across the cañon. We then insisted that the newcomers join us, and hurried on toward the feast.

A quarter of a mile beyond the stream, we came upon a small group of shacks. One of them, more pretentious than the rest, was nearly twelve feet square, and had a floor of split bamboo. From all appearances, it had weathered about two rainy seasons, and could stand about one more.

The owner of the house must have been a mighty hunter and trapper, for a small tree in front was hung with his trophies. A score of monkey skulls grinned at us from the ends of the smaller branches, and from the larger limbs dangled the lower jaws of more than a dozen boars, their large tusks glistening in the evening sun. Hanging below several of these jaws, were bamboo spearheads, similar to those we had seen in the traps, and all darkened with bloodstains. There were also the jaw-bones of a number of deer hanging about the tree, but strange to say, no antlers. These, perhaps, were found useful in too many ways to permit of their being kept as trophies.

Among the grass shelters surrounding the main shack, fires were burning and food cooking in crude vessels, but as far as the eye could reach, no human being was in sight. Neither was there a sound to break the ominous and decidedly uncomfortable silence. It was as though we had dropped in as unwelcome guests at the feast of some mountain goblins, and that the offended spirits had vanished into the air upon our arrival, but were still about, planning our undoing. A breeze sighed through the branches of the trophy tree, the monkey skulls nodded derisively and leered at us from their empty eye-sockets.

We all felt the need of a little noise, so we called upon Lucas. He and one of the newly-acquired Negritos were directed to call in the natives, and their yells soon convinced us that the welkin was in perfectly good ringing order. Meanwhile, we kept the rest of our Negritos close around us, lest some over-nervous brave might let loose an arrow from his hiding place to find its way between our ribs.

Up from the grass around us rose the dark bodies of naked

men, each with a broad-headed arrow fitted to the string of his long *palma brava* bow. Again we were inspired with a supreme desire to look peaceful, and we made haste to call the chief and tell him so. Of course, this message had to be conveyed to him with the proper amount of dignity befitting those of our exalted station condescending to commune with a primitive savage. By the time our remarks percolated through Andres, our interpreting boy, they amounted to something like this: "The *Americanos distinguidos* say that they are not going to bother you, that is to say, not unless you displease them. They have even given permission for you to continue your fies-

ta, and have come to make a greater fiesta. They want to see your fiesta, and are going to camp here; and they want you to build them a bamboo shelter with a grass roof; and you must build it quickly, because it is nearly dark."

This speech seemed to allay all suspicions in their simple minds; and half an hour later, the shack was built, the women and children had been brought back from their hiding places in the grass, and the celebration took up exactly where it had left off.

Like most mountain people, these tiny savages apparently have their feuds. We had scarcely gotten settled, when a slight commotion revealed the fact that one of the Negritos whom Lucas had brought along was in some sort of trouble. He was surrounded by a group of armed warriors, and was wildly gesticulating, talking and pleading to as stonily relentless a bunch of faces as I have ever seen.

"What are you going to do?" I asked the chief. "Kill him," was the reply. "What has he done?" I inquired. "Nothing." "Then why are you going to kill him?" "Because he is the brother of Casillo.

We want to kill Casillo, but can't catch him, so we are going to kill his brother who will do just as well."

"Very good," I replied, "This boy is easy to catch, and you can kill him some other time. But you must not kill him now, because we want to use him. He is one of our cargadores, and if you killed him he could not carry our stuff."

To a brain scarcely fertile enough to nourish the roots of a shock of kinky hair, this seemed a thoroughly reasonable argument, and the killing was postponed. Moreover, to our great surprise, it was found that an hour later the incident had been sufficiently forgotten for Casillo's brother to take a leading part in the festivities.

One of the chief's first acts was to line up his four sons, and after announcing very proudly that they were his, he pointed to his own features and then to theirs, calling our attention to a resemblance which left the matter of their paternity entirely beyond doubt. In having so many sons, he was particularly fortunate among his fellows; for poor food and shelter, dirt, the prevalence of skin diseases and a nomadic life are gradually but effectively thinning the ranks of his race.

Even before the advent of the Spanish, a Chinese trader wrote of these people as being very remarkable, and by way of illustration, mentioned that they had round eyes, and small families, two equally astounding facts to a Chinaman.

Whenever Dame Fashion has nothing more than a gee-string to deal with sartorially, she usually takes to some form of altering the anatomy by way of producing a modish effect. The chief's sons were in the height of fashion. With a sharp piece of bamboo, rows of wounds had been gouged in their chests, so that each was decorated with sufficient scars to make him beautiful.

These, the chief explained, had the further virtue of keeping off disease. The cure for disease was even worse than the preventative. A number of these little people had their arms and shoulders covered with what appeared to be large vaccination scars. These people, the chief said, had been sick, and had holes burned into the flesh of their arms with coals of fire in order to drive out the devil of sickness. Even the weakest patient is said to become very lively under this treatment.

Besides scarifying the chest, another popular form of adornment was that of sharpening the front teeth. This, I was informed, was done by chipping off the corners with a bolo, and then finishing the job by filing with a piece of rough sand stone - think about this the next time you sit in a dentist's chair.

Just what this fiesta was all about, I was not fully able to find out, but apparently it had something to do with giving thanks for the food which the gods had provided. At any rate, small quantities of food were placed on banana leaves, and set on a bamboo stand around which the Negritos danced, one or two at a time. They would solemnly approach the food, gesticulate in a slow and respectful manner, and break into a chant, their little flat feet all the while keeping perfect time with the "music." This latter was a sort of two-note tum-tum coming from an instrument not unlike a tiny, crude-looking, flat guitar. When the fingers of one musician became numb from playing, he would hand the instrument to another who would sometimes vary the monotony by playing two notes which were different from those twanged by his predecessor.

Some of the dancers showed great exuberance of spirits; others hopped about with ludicrous solemnity. There were two who might have been termed professionals and who danced for the amusement of the crowd, clapping their hands, slapping their thighs and kicking higher than any of the others.

Many of their dances told stories in excellent pantomime. The *camote* dance, after a little hopping about by way of warming up, went through all of the motions of planting, guarding, digging, cooking and eating a crop of these native sweet potatoes. All through the pantomime, the feet of the dancer kept up a hop-kick, heel-and-toe motion in perfect time. A final smack of the lips, in token of the good taste of the *camotes*, brought great glee to the spectators, and caused many eyes to roll in the direction of the fires where some of the women were cooking. In the wild boar dance, the performer alternately took the parts of the hunter and the beast, and wound up by lying on his back, kicking up into the air and squealing, illustrative of the death of the boar by the hunter's last arrow.

As the three of us sat on a log among these tiny men, averaging scarcely more than four and a half feet in height, and women even smaller, I could not help recalling an old picture I had seen, when a small boy, of Du Chaillu among the Pygmies. How I had envied Du Chaillu at the time, and how my boyish imagination had reveled in the weird antics of those African counterparts of the Negritos. And here I was, as though transported by some fairy to the land of my childish dreams.

Hunter, who with Hooper had accompanied me, passed around a box of cigarettes, and men, women and children alike took them and began to smoke. Some, more frugal than the rest, broke theirs in two and stored the unused halves in the folds of their gee-strings for future use, but all smoked, and did so backwards. After lighting their cigarettes in the normal way, they turned them around and smoked with the lighted end in their mouths. How they avoided burning their tongues or filling their mouths with ashes, I don't know, but somehow they managed to enjoy their smoke.

After dark, the religious factor in the fiesta took decided turn toward frenzied fanaticism. The chanting became louder, the contortions wilder and more violent. The firelight glistened on sweating bodies and threw huge shadows like leaping demons beyond every dancer. Before the sacred food they tossed themselves to

146

and fro, until many sank in a faint from sheer exhaustion, only to struggle to their feet later and renew this fanatical performance.

Hooper, at the other end of the log upon which I was sitting, was using Andres as an interpreter, and trying valiantly to find out what it was all about, what the gods were doing, what became of departed spirits, who made it rain, what happened when it thundered and the best method of avoiding the devils. However, by the time the delirious ravings of frenzied savages had been translated from a broken Zambal dialect into English by a Pampangan who had no idea what the conversation was intended to bring out, and whose English was scantier than his clothes, Hooper's deductions on the subject of Negrito theology remained in rather nebular form.

In spite of all the hubbub and excitement, our hike of considerably more than twenty miles through the mountains that day, soon began to weigh heavily upon our eyelids and we crawled under the mosquito bars in our shelter fifty yards down the hill and were soon asleep. Throughout the whole night, whenever I awoke, I could see the yellow flicker of firelight, and hear the tumtum of the musical instrument, the sound of voices, sometimes festive and sometimes in weird chant.

CHAPTER XX

Stuffed Dog - The Legend of Mariveles - Happy Thoughts of Sizzling Corpses – The Head-Chopping Party

For a year, I had been lured by the hope of taking the Southern Island trip, a jaunt with all the features of a ten-day yachting voyage through comic opera, set under colorful skies in a paradise of south sea beauty. At last, I had my orders, and was impatiently awaiting the Liscum's next sailing.

Twice each month, the transport made the round of southern army posts, carrying supplies and such troops as were traveling under orders; and along with them, the jovial group of joy-riders who were getting away from routine, and making a floating house party out of dinner, got acquainted, stretched ourselves in easy chairs on deck, and hob-knobbed in little groups on the trip ahead of us. To our left, lay Cavite, with all its luscious mangoes, where Aguinaldo now peacefully farmed after stirring days of his insurrectionary activities. In the long, low shoreline, there was no sign of that far-famed mountain of gold that had lured the early Chinese voyagers in quest of its treasures. These had searched Cavite, had failed to be rewarded, and had stopped right there. It was only an enterprising American who had eventually discovered this gold-yielding piece of terrain, and it was not in Cavite at all.

In the Benguet Mountains, a hundred miles north of Manila, there lived a tribe of gee-stringed, head-hunting mountaineers, similar to the Dayaks of Borneo. They were known to possess little flakes and nuggets of gold, to make these into earrings and bracelets, and among other things, to be extremely fond of dogs, particularly when the latter were roasted.

Our enterprising American made a bee line for the home of these Igorots and their gold, but he could get no one to tell him where the shiny metal came from. Not being able to go to the mountain of gold, he decided to bring the mountain to him. His first thought was to exchange dogs for nuggets; but here again he was disappointed, by finding an already well-established dog market at Baguio, against which he could not compete. But even this did not find him at the end of his rope.

Like most heathen people untouched by higher civilization, the Igorots were truthful, honest, and expected others to be equally so - a failing which has always led them to suffer at the hands of their more enlightened brethren. They liked ornaments, and bright metals, and they were not skillful craftsmen, so the way was clear to our enterprising American.

Word went out through the mountains that for its weight in ordinary nuggets and scales of gold, a white man was exchanging beautiful shiny silver discs with wonderful pictures on both sides of them. They could be strung together into bracelets, suspended from the neck, or, hung from the ears by wires. The nuggets poured in, as bags of new silver pesos, worth fifty cents apiece, were taken up the Baguio trail; and before the unsuspicious Igorot could be better informed, the American had gone with his fortune.

However, there is little need of feeling sorry for them. The gold meant nothing to them, they got more pleasure out of the silver, and continued to enjoy their dog feasts none the less.

I shall never forget the anxiety which I felt for an Airedale which I once took on a hunting trip through the Igorot country, wondering all the while how the axiom "Love me, love my dog," was going to turn out. Not only did I fear the loss of my pup, but thoughts of the labor-saving method whereby the Igorot prepares his feast were particularly distasteful to me.

When one of these canine celebrations is to take place, a lean, native cur is tied up for days without food, until its sunken flanks show the poor creature to be on the point of starvation. When, like a gift from Heaven, a great bowl of rice is placed before it, and it is allowed to eat, as only a famished cur can.

One by one, its wrinkles are smoothed out, its skin tightens, and its once hollow sides bulge with replete convexity. It licks its chops, wags its tail, takes a deep breath and stiffly turns around before lying down for a nap. Having filled itself to capacity, it is then tapped on the head, roasted and served, its stuffing of rice being particularly prized for a flavor which is said to be most deliciously doggy.

It was well after dark when we were opposite Mariveles Mountain, and passed through the chain of fortified islands which protected the mouth of the harbor. Corregidor, with its tiers of batteries, loomed up like a Gibraltar, as the broad beam of one of its searchlights swept past us, and illuminated the open stretches of water. Beyond, were the smaller islands of Fraile (the Friar), Caballo (The Horse) and Carabao.

There is a legend that, way back in the early Spanish times, a certain indecorous affair took place, which resulted in the naming of the mountain, and these islands. Like most legends, you can hear it told in half a dozen ways, but in the main, the stories differ little, and all agree that the incident was thoroughly scandalous.

The trouble was started by the *fraile*, who, in most unecclesiastical fashion, became enamored of Maria Vélez a nun - in fact, a very beautiful nun. Maria had just come over from Mexico.

She was seventeen, and having reached the age of indiscretion, proceeded to be indiscreet. Along with Mr. Fraile, she eloped, and went to the mouth of Manila Bay, where next day the two elected to catch a Spanish galleon which was sailing for Mexico.

Unfortunately for the lovers, the sailing of the galleon was delayed, and meanwhile, *el corregidor*, the magistrate, was hot on their trail. Some say that *caballo* and a carabao figured in the chase, and some say they didn't; but at any rate, the pair was caught at the foot of the mountain, where they had vainly waited the galleon. Maria, with her clothing torn to rags, lay half fainting on the beach; and the *fraile* sat nearby, wounded and bleeding after a fight with natives who had tried to take her away.

Think of how the tongues of ancient Manila gossips wagged, and of how often the name of Maria Vélez was cackled when seedy eyes were turned toward the mountain sky. No wonder that this soon became Mariveles Mountain and that the Fraile and Corregidor were nearby - and Maria, poor girl, was sent back to a convent in Mexico; while the sinful *fraile* was ordered to go as a missionary and teach morals to the benighted Visayans.

All next day we followed the coast of Luzon, threading our way along smaller islands, many of them tiny dome-shaped affairs, covered with green vegetation and undercut twenty or thirty feet by the waves, so as to give them the appearance of huge mushrooms sticking up out of the water.

Try as I would, I could not keep my mind or my eyes off of Mindoro. There was something gripping in the appearance of its rugged shores rising sheer from the sea, its dark clothing of heavy forests, and its peaks boldly piercing the sky, and disputing its possession with the clouds. In those very hills were *tamarao*, the vicious mountain buffalo, found in no other part of the world; and a hunter who followed one of its swampy valleys might be rewarded by a wild carabao head with a five or six-foot spread of horns. Then, there were primitive Manguyan tribes, with their tales of the strange white natives that were sometimes seen wandering some twenty or thirty miles inland. There were yarns, too, of a great swamp of oil, of streams where gold was mixed with the pebbles, and all the other stories that usually circulate about an almost inaccessible country. Twice I had planned to cross the island, but on both occasions something had interfered. Now, that I was so near to it, the sight of it whetted further my already keen desire to explore its almost untouched interior.

For another night, the Liscum glided through phosphorescent waters, and at dawn next morning, we awoke to find ourselves tied up alongside of a volcano. From the sandy beach which swept in crescent shape around the harbor of Legaspi, Mayon rose in a cone of beautiful symmetry, till its cratered summit towered twice the height of Vesuvius. Veiled in a soft mist of floating clouds, the mountain slept, and in the beauty of its tranquil slumber, men had forgotten the awful fury of its waking hours - forgotten the violence of its terrific explosions, the midnight darkness under its clouds of ashes, the fiery column of molten hell spurting from its crater and the charred bones of thousands who lay buried around its base. New villages have each time sprung up where the old ones were destroyed; and though scarcely more than a quarter of a century has passed since brimstone rained from a blackened sky and houses blazed on the slopes on Mayon, the next shower will find as many thatched roofs as ever to fall upon.

Like all joy-riders, we went out to gloat over the remains of old Daraga, which had been destroyed by the eruption of 1814. Here we feasted our imagination upon pleasant thoughts of a mountain gone mad, and spouting fire upon the sizzling bodies of men and women who writhed in the last agonies of a terrible death. The delightful way in which people gather around a pool of blood where someone has been murdered, revel in the eyehooks and crushing tongs of a collection of ancient instruments of torture, or gather as souvenirs from a battlefield, bullets which have flattened against the bones of their countrymen, shows a truly refreshing phase in the make-up of civilized man.

Very little remains of old Daraga except the upper part of the Spanish church, now a mass of ruins with grass and bushes sprouting from its broken walls. For a time it served as a hiding-place for a group of *insurrectos*, who plotted mischief in a half-buried room under the tower; but a little row of bamboo crosses at the entrance to this room, is eloquent of the result of their plotting.

When we had walked long enough in the tracks of devastation, we turned to the palm-bordered avenues that led through the army post, met and talked with old friends, and were back on the boat by sailing time.

A day later we piled out on the familiar old dock at Cebú. It was all just as I had left it - the long line of carabao carts, hauling hemp and copra to be loaded into a waiting steamer; boys with pearls of various colors in cotton-lined pill-boxes, offering them for sale and lowering the prices steadily as the sailing hour drew near; a row of *tartanillas* awaiting the passenger who would climb in, shake the sleeping driver and say, "*Sique*," officers of the garrison down to meet the joy-riders with invitations to dinner - everything including the smell of coconut oil and tuba, was there, unchanged.

In rattling vehicles, we passed the old shrine where Magellan held his first mass on the island, clattered down the main street, which bears the famous navigator's name, and wandered for some hours about the town.

Along toward four in the afternoon, small groups began to gather on the balcony of the club, which overhung the water and was within a hundred yards of the Liscum. It was a cool, indolent sort of a place where we could loll in reclining chairs and make the last half hour pass easily.

Someone was in the midst of telling an interesting yarn, when the Liscum's whistle sounded its message to hurry - a message which is happily ignored wherever bananas grow. When the yarn was finished, and the group was leisurely starting on its way, when Capt. Barclay's bulk appeared on the bridge of his vessel, and an ultimatum thundered from the depths of his huge chest: "If you people don't get on board damned quick, this ship is going to sail without you!"

When we had once more settled ourselves on deck, I found that Hardigan, of Manila, had gotten on. I was interested in seeing him because of a famous head-chopping party described to me by a Mr. Stanley. Stanley told me Hardigan had been the hero in this incident. I had last seen Stanley in Manila.

"Have you heard about Hardigan's party in Hongkong?" [sic] he asked.

I had not.

"Well," he said, "He and a few others here had been pretty well tied down to their offices through the dry season, and decided

154

they needed a rest; so the whole bunch piled onto a steamer for Hongkong, and started to pull off a real jollification. They must have done pretty well, because from what I hear, they left a trail of empty champagne bottles all the way across the China Sea.

"After they had kept up their celebration for a couple of days in Hongkong, they decided that they wanted to see an execution. The Chinamen up there have a way of chopping off heads for almost any kind of an offense, so the bunch went around to the jail to see if anything was doing. They looked up the executioner, and found him to be a regular giant of a man with the most terrible-looking face they had ever seen. Any Chinaman who had ever laid eyes on him would hesitate more than once before committing a crime. Somehow, he had picked up a little English.

"'Chop head off today?' asked Hardigan.

"'No can do today.' he replied. `Come back thlee days, choppy thlee heads!'

"This, of course, didn't suit Hardigan, because he expected to be gone from Hongkong before the three days were up; so he reached in his pocket and pulled out a twenty-peso bill and said, `Maybe so can do now.'"

"The executioner eyed the bill a minute, put it in his pocket and said, `Can do.' Then he went into the jail for about long enough to give the jailer a rake-off on the twenty pesos, and came out dragging three of the most dilapidated-looking Chinamen they had ever seen.

"With three whacks of his beheading sword, the executioner separated these fellows from their heads; whereupon, he bowed toward Hardigan, smiled and retired.

Naturally, I was anxious to hear all about this from Hardigan, first hand, so I joined him on deck, where he sat comfortably stretched in a steamer chair.

"I heard you are an expert on Chinese executions," I ventured.

155

"Executions?" he answered.

"Yes," I said, "How about the head-chopping party up in Hongkong? You must have had a great time on that trip."

"No," he replied, "I wasn't along, but I heard all about it afterwards."

"You know," I continued, "I had gotten the idea that you were one of the leading lights in that expedition."

"No," he assured me, "I didn't go. The ring leader of that outfit was a fellow from Manila named Stanley."

Chapter XXI

Moros - Mule-skinners - The Rotund Nudity of the Pompous Major - The Treasure.

The sun's first rays fell upon the red and yellow sails of Moro *vintas*, the throbbing sounds in the Liscum's engine room died out, there was the clatter and jangle of a steam winch on deck, some volcanic noises from the Captain, and we sidled up to the end of the pier at Camp Overton. Glistening in the dew of early morning, lay Mindanao, an island where the name of the Prophet is spoken in reverence, where it is immoral to eat anything that the shadow of an infidel has fallen upon, where heaven is the reward for killing a Christian, and where a man may have wives to his heart's content - that is, if many wives is contenting to the heart.

There was none of that garrulous crowd of curious natives which usually hung about the dock to watch the boat come in. True enough, there were Moros about, Moros with blackened teeth, with long hair wrapped around their heads and bound by colored turbans, with short jackets, sashes and baggy red or purple trousers - but all were going somewhere or doing something, not loitering to gape at any white man.

There is something that you can't help admiring about the entire independence of one of these Mohammedan Malays. He cringes, caters or kowtows to no man, and he looks you straight in the eye in a way which says very clearly that as far as he is concerned, you can go to the devil. He is savage, fearless, and revels in a good fight; and with it all, he dresses like a peacock, is a real artist in his brass-work and wood-carving, and can step into any club and, beat the best of us in a game of chess.

His favorite weapon is a *kampilan*, a sort of two-handed cross between a sword and a cleaver. He carries it in a scabbard made of two pieces of wood, tied together with a grass string. This, he finds very convenient, since he can carry his *kampilan* on his shoulder while passing you on a trail, and can cut right through the grass string and deftly remove your head, without giving you warning by drawing his weapon from its scabbard. Consequently, it has often been found rather impolitic to wander alone on the out-of-the-way paths of this part of Mindanao.

At Overton is the beginning of the famous Keithley trail, which leads to Lake Lanao and Camps Keithley. From the earliest times, the Lanao Moros have been fighters, and there is not a mile of the trail which has not seen bloodshed. Spaniard and American alike have been ambushed, attacked and killed along its course, but every white man slain has been paid for many times over in dead Moros.

There is only one thing that has a wholesome bluff over the Lanao Moro, and that is a pack train. When Keithley was first garrisoned by our troops, all supplies were carried up on the backs of pack-mules, heavily guarded by soldiers. As things settled down, the guards grew smaller, and finally nothing was left but the civilian packers. When the Moros noticed this, they at once started something. Shots were fired and spears thrown at the packers whenever they went by, and from time to time, a man was chopped up.

Men who can speak convincingly to mules, are rarely of a gentle and shrinking disposition, and these packers were no exception. Being civilians, they were also unhampered by the strict orders which kept the soldiers in check. Consequently, these burly mule-skinners decided to do what they called "putting the fear of God into the Moros." From then on, the packers took a pot shot at every living thing that could be seen from the trail. After the second trip, the pack trains had the trail all to themselves; and when the tinkle of the bell on the leading mare of each string of mules was heard coming, every Moro cleared out. Even to this day, a man walking all the way from Overton to Keithley will never lay eyes on a Moro if he rings a bell as he walks.

Around Keithley, the Moro *datos* have nearly always made trouble. Until very recently, they have considered themselves entirely independent. They have fortified themselves in their strongly entrenched cottas, have defied our troops, and forced us to attack them under conditions most favorable to the kind of warfare practiced by these Malay feudal barons.

One *dato*, finding time hanging rather heavily on his hands, sent a message to the commander at Keithley to this general effect:

"I am fortified in my cotta, and have enough men and arms to kill anything you can send after me. Come and get me if you dare."

Along with the message, he sent the head of an American soldier recently killed by the Moros. Such an appeal could not be resisted, and the messenger was hastened back with a reply: "You can expect us next Saturday."

To the *dato's* misfortune, this was exactly what he expected; and when a column of troops, instead of waiting until Saturday, arrived on Tuesday, he was caught napping and captured.

As the Moros quieted down, Keithley came to be regarded as a very pleasant post, except when it rained - and it usually rained. Officers lived there with their families, invited their Manila friends down to visit them, and provided them with umbrellas when they got there.

Nearly every house had a shower bath, consisting of a water barrel and spout, set up over a split bamboo floor through which the water trickled down to the ground several feet below. One of these light bamboo floors proved the undoing of a very pompous, as well as decidedly rotund, old major. The siesta hour was just over, when a garrulous group down from Manila on a house party passed by the major's house. This portly gentleman was at the time refreshing himself with a shower. Just as he was entirely engrossed in enjoyment of the cool water, the floor gave way under the strain of his weight, and dropped him into full view of the house party - that is to say, full view except for his head, which still remained above the floor. He made frantic efforts to climb back up through the hole, but the sharp ends of the broken bamboo strips pointed downward like so many spears. He could not come out from under the house and enter by the door, without rushing through the giggling, blushing crowd from the house party. Meanwhile, he had gotten his eyes full of soap, and stood wildly yelling for his boy, who at length came to the rescue with a bath robe. The major was not seen again for a week.

Just before our boat sailed, an old Moro came down to the dock to sell rings and silver ornaments. His hair was gray, his leathery face was lined with deep furrows, and he wore a Moro mustache, the only kind that he could grow. Above the corners of his mouth were two spots, each about the size of a butter bean, which could be coaxed to sprout a few whiskers, and these hairs, after long and careful training, had grown sufficiently in length to give him the general appearance of some sort of a bug with long feelers.

He had evidently had a good day of it, for when I passed him, nearly all of his things had been sold. As I went by, he held out a ring. The intricate delicacy of its design, and the excellence of its workmanship would have been a credit to any goldsmith; yet the old fellow had made it himself, without education and with the crudest of implements.

"Buy *singsing*?" he asked.

I stopped for a moment, and asked him if he had any others.

"No," he replied, "no got *otro singing*," combining in a sentence of four words, the three languages of English, Spanish and Moro.

Another day, and the long line of our wake stretched well into the Sulu Sea. There was a warm, voluptuous softness to the Southern breeze, something gratifying to the senses, yet in no way productive of languor. It seemed to rouse the imagination, to stir up thoughts of treasure ships, pirates, romance and gold. We watched every palm-covered island, half expecting to see a long racy craft glide out from behind it, with a skull at her masthead and a cloud of white spray at her bow.

From pirates, our talk drifted to treasures - a rather short drift after all. A naval officer was sitting next to me.

"When I was here on my first cruise," he said, "I ran across the greatest treasure in this part of the world, and it's probably here yet. I was a youngster, just out of the Naval Academy, and found out that I could get pearls from these Moro fishermen for almost nothing. I wanted enough to make string for, - well, never mind what for. Anyhow, I wanted some pearls, and managed to get some very good ones.

"While I was getting my pearls, an old Moro told me that on an island near Jolla, there was a jewel which was the most wonderful on earth. I tried to get him to describe it, but all he could say was that years ago, it had been found on the seashore, that it had been treasured by the Moros on that island, not only as a gem of incalculable value, but as a sacred talisman as well, and that nowhere in the world was there anything like it.

"I told the Captain about it, and he was as anxious to see the thing as I was, so he took our destroyer down toward Jolla and got in touch with the dato who kept the treasure. At first, the old fellow flatly refused to let us see it, but after sufficient bribery, he reluctantly consented. However, he wished to take no chances on our making away with the jewel, so he insisted that the two of us come alone to his house, where we might see the gem under proper guard. This sounded a little as though the dato had ideas of

161

chopping us up, so we insisted that we could not, with dignity, travel without our customary retinue.

"Finally, the thing was arranged. With ten armed men, we were to meet the dato at the stockade around his house. He, with an equal number of his warriors, was then to bring out the treasure and let us see it.

"Well, we got there, and found the old fellow ready for us. I never saw such formality in my life. Our sailors were lined up on one side, looking like a bunch of arsenals, and the dato's men opposite them with enough cutlery to carve up an army. In the middle, the dato and his umbrella-bearer met us and said that he was ready. Then he beckoned toward his men, and from behind them two Moros came out carrying a carved *nara* chest with huge brass hinges. They set this down beside the dato, and retired.

"Another man then came out, all dressed up like a rainbow, and stood in front of the dato. The dato nodded to him, and he opened the carved casket, took out a small ebony box, inlaid with silver, and put it on top of the chest. Then, with an air of great reverence, he raised the lid. Before us lay the jewel - the glass eye of a French doll."

CHAPTER XXII

The Sultan of Sulu - The Boat That Went Wild
The Expert - The Last Whiff

Covered with booths and strange-looking houses, swarming with slant-eyed, crafty-looking men, sleek, pajamad young women and leathery, silent old hags, the Chinese pier jutted out toward us as we approached the dock at Jolo. The truth will never be known about that pier. If it were, there would doubtless be hangings galore. Many who have wandered out upon it have never come back; the smell of opium permeates its ancient timbers; smuggled goods are bought and sold in its booths; corpses have floated out from under it with the tide. As you pass it, you can catch the odor of joss sticks burning before heathen images, you can hear the jangle of discordant music, but the old pier tells no tales, and the eternal mystery of its goings on remains as one of those Oriental enigmas which baffle the prying curiosity of the West.

A JOLO MOUNT

When off the boat, the whole atmosphere of Jolo was suggestive of colorful pageantry and jaunty make-believe. It gave you the feeling of having been dropped into some gay and picturesque land of your fancy, where every scene was cunningly devised for beauty, and every event a pleasing bit of drama.

Facing me, as I walked off of the transport, was the massive wall of an old fortification. Oddly shaped trees were scattered about on the grass-plot in front of it, flowering vines clung here and there to its crumbling stones, and moss marked its crevices with a lattice-work of green. In the center of the wall, was an archway decorated with weathered carvings, and through it, opened a gate of heavy iron.

For a long time, I stood looking at the whole scene and wondering where I had run across it before. It had a strange, haunting familiarity, like something that had come to me in a dream, and yet I could not place it. I had a feeling that off to the left there ought to be a tree. I looked, and there it was, just as I had expected. While I was puzzling about it, a procession slowly approached and moved past the gate with a solemn, pompous dignity not wholly without a touch of the ludicrous. There were perhaps twenty Moros in the procession, most of them armed with silver-mounted *barongs* and wavy-edged *krises* [swords]. Their slender legs were clothed to the ankle in skin-tight trousers, close-fitting jackets with buttons of gold and silver reached to their waists, gaudy sashes were wound about their bodies, and colored turbans covered all but the tops of their heads. Some were old, grave and wise-looking; others, young, alert, lithe and fierce. One carried a large two-handed fan, and another held up an elaborately ornate umbrella of crimson cloth. Under the umbrella walked a small, inconspicuous man in a fez. It was none other than His Worshipful Majesty, Haroun Narassid, Descendant of the Prophet, and Sultan of Sulu.

Suddenly, the whole thing flashed on my memory. It was the same old wall, the same gateway, costumes, umbrella and all that I had seen years before in the stage-setting of George Ade's play. I had enjoyed it all in comic opera, and here it was again.

Despite the pomp and glory of the Sultan's court, his temporal power has, nevertheless, been much curtailed. He is kept in office by our Government, and also receives a salary from the British, as the result of his authority over some of their subjects. His real function is that of religious head of all the Moros of the Sulu Archipelago and Borneo. He is supreme arbiter in the matter of religious derelictions and can impose penalties upon his subjects for conduct incompatible with the teachings of Mohammed. Since the Prophet's teachings cover almost everything, and the penalties usually take the form of fines, the Sultan, as a rule, manages to live fairly well.

The Sultan's mother, being ambitious for him, is said to have murdered his half-brother, the rightful heir to the throne, so that her own son might become Sultan. In all probability, he will be the last to reign, for even with his four wives, he has no children; and upon his death, the throne of that picturesque potentate will become vacant forever.

"This must be an occasion of state," said a voice beside me. I turned to see one of my fellow-passengers.

"The last time I saw the Sultan dolled up like that was the day Jingle Wilson had his head chopped pretty nearly off, and John Kennedy got slashed across the temple with a *barong*."

"How did that happen?" I asked.

"We'd been chasing the old outlaw Jikiri after he had plundered and murdered everything he could get his hands on, and we got word that Archie Miller's outfit had finally cornered him and some of his men in a cave. The Sultan wanted to show that he was with us in putting down outlaws and decided to help; so he got an automatic pistol, his umbrella and fan-bearer and all of his court, and came out to watch us from a safe distance.

"Well, we fiddled around about three days in as mean a place as I have ever tried to fight in. The sun just about broiled us during the day, and at night the mosquitoes ate us up. We couldn't shoot into the openings of the cave without getting up close, and we couldn't get close without losing men. In all, the Moros managed to pick off over twenty.

"Old Jikiri swore that he would die fighting and he did a good job of it. If we had some grenades, we could have made short work of him, but we didn't have any to throw. Finally, some of the officers got pretty well disgusted with the way things were going, and decided it was time for the finish. John Kennedy, with nothing but his pistol, crawled into one entrance of the cave. There were some shots, and flashes of steel, and John rolled over with a gash that pretty nearly fixed him.

"Wilson and some of the others were by this time at another entrance, when the Moros came out like a bunch of wild cats. Of course, the Moros didn't last long, but while Wilson was emptying his pistol into one, another gave him a slash across the neck that no ordinary man would have recovered from. A month later, however, we propped Jingle up on some pillows in the hospital, and he wrote home, saying, `My head is growing back nicely. `Things grow rapidly in the tropics.'"

Along with several of the Liscum's passengers, I dined that day with the American Governor of Jolo. Our host went to some pains to tell us how quiet, peaceful and law-abiding his Moros had become - an assurance which can always be counted on from the ruler of any turbulent province. Nevertheless, an officer of the Jolo garrison, sitting next to me, suggested that if I went outside of the walled part of town, I had better go armed.

SULTAN OF JOLO & HIS CHIEFS

"Pretty nearly any time," he said, "you are likely to run into a *juramentado*. Every now and then, some old Moro gets bored with

166

life, and decides that flouncing around with the beautiful houris [virgins] of the seventh heaven is preferable to his present lot. His shortest cut to the seventh heaven is to die killing infidels, so he goes before his priest, shaves off his eyebrows, swears a mighty oath, whets his barong to a razor edge, and comes to town.

"He hangs around looking for a bunch of Christians, and when the opportune time comes, he whips out his barong and hacks until someone finishes him. It hasn't been a month since a juramentado ran amuck in the market, and accounted for five men before he was killed. A sentinel shot him four times through the body before he was even off his feet. Moros take a lot of killing before they quit.

"We don't have much of it, now that the Sultan and his *datos* work with us and don't encourage it, but for a while during the old Spanish times it got to be such a fad that the seventh heaven and the Spanish cemetery were pretty nearly overrun. After a lot of Spaniards had been killed, the Governor sent for the Sultan and told him that it was up to him to take the necessary means to put a stop to it. The Sultan said that he had the warmest friendship for the Spanish, and deplored the fact that his people were going juramentado, but said that to his great regret this was a form of religious fanaticism over which he had no control. That very afternoon, another member of the garrison was killed.

"The next morning, a Spanish gunboat started down the Jolo coast and shot up everything within range of the shore. The Sultan came rushing to the Governor with a protest that his towns were being destroyed and innocent people who were at peace with Spain were being shot down by the score. The Governor listened politely and expressed his regret, saying that while he deplored the incident, it was, nevertheless, a form of religious fanaticism over which he had no control. The gunboat had gone juramentado. The rest of the Governor's administration was peaceful."

After dinner, I strapped on a .45 pistol and wandered around among slender-legged, hard-faced Moros, carefully eying each one who approached to be sure that he had eyebrows. Everywhere were sentinels armed with short riot guns loaded with buckshot. Some of these were Moro constabulary, who were recruited from the Lanao or Zamboanga country, and who could relish a fight even with Moros, as long as they did not come from their own district.

A constabulary officer told me that a couple of days before, one of his men had come to him to borrow five pesos until next payday, and had brought one of his wives to be left as a security. However, with a five-peso Moro wife in the house, he did not feel entirely secure, so declined the soldier's offer.

No one goes to Jolo without visiting the shop of Chino Charley. This smiling Celestial has very much of a way with him, when it comes to selling you things you don't want. Of course, I had to buy some Jolo lanterns - everybody did - and when I boarded the Liscum, I had two beauties of oiled silk and bamboo to hang on my porch. Ever since, I have been carting about these huge, lovely, artistic nuisances.

As we left Jolo, Bud Dajo, the mountain where the hostile Moros had made their last important stand against our troops, topped the sky-line. In its crater, now a hemp plantation, twelve hundred of them fortified themselves, refused to surrender, and fought a desperate struggle until not one was left alive. With rifles, shot guns, spears, barongs, krises, and huge boulders, they stubbornly opposed our men on the steep slopes of their last citadel. In the final charge, when our men broke into their works, many upon being struck with bayonets seized the end of the soldier's rifle, and pulled the weapon further through their own bodies, in order that they might be close enough to deal a last dying blow with their barongs. As a desperate fighter, the Sulu Moro can take his place among the best.

Our next stop was at Zamboanga, a brief stop, to be sure, but a most pleasant one. We mingled with the garrison, visited the Spanish fort and had a luncheon at the Club. No one can visit Zamboanga without enjoying the tranquil beauty of its gardens and palm groves; no one can be stationed there without carrying away happy memories.

We were now well started on our return voyage to Manila. At Parang, another post in Mindanao, we had to take on a battalion of Visayan scouts, who were changing station. This gave us some hours, so several of us got the quartermaster's launch and went up the Cottabato River to the town of Cottabato, where everyone usually loaded up with Moro brass. This district, which had formerly been the scene of heavy fighting, was now lightly garrisoned and peaceful enough.

Dato Piang, the head man in Cottabato, had always been on good terms with the Americans, but his son-in-law, Dato Ali, has made a lot of trouble. Piang now runs a "saw-mill," consisting of a large number of men, sawing planks from logs by means of hand saws. Among other original characteristics, he has a bamboo ear. At some time during a career which landed him as ruler of his people, Piang had differences which resulted in a whack at his head with a *kampilan*. The blade struck him above the temple, slashed downwards close to the skull, and took off a flap of flesh, including an ear, which hung down against his neck.

After this little difference was settled, Piang bandaged the flap back to his head, where it proceeded to grow. Unfortunately, however, he was a little off in his idea of where the flap ought to go, and wound up with an ear which served nothing but ornamental purposes, and a small hole in the side of his head where his misguided ear should have been. Ever since, he has worn a bamboo ear-trumpet in the hole, and swears that he can hear through it better than ever.

On the way down the river, I fell into conversation with an old scout officer.

"It's a lot quieter down here now than it was the first time I took this trip," he said. "I was on my way to Jolo about the time the civil government took over this province from the military authorities. Things were a long way from being settled at the time, but we had on board the transport a new civil official of some sort who was going to straighten everything out.

"He told me that the whole trouble lay in the fact that there was no one in the army who really knew how to handle Moros; but that he was an expert on non-Christian tribes, and understood the workings of the Moro mind. He said it took a man who had made a study of the non-Christian point of view to handle the situation, and that he had investigated the whole proposition from a scientific standpoint, and would have the Moros quiet within a month.

"Well," continued the scout officer, "the transport went on down to Jolo, and on the way back stopped again near the mouth of the Cottabato river. Some men brought a long box up the gangway and laid it on deck. It contained the expert on non-Christian tribes."

A lively scene awaited us on our return to Parang. The lower decks of the Liscum were a maze of khaki uniforms, red calico skirts, chicken coops, green and yellow *panuelos*, bundles tied up in banana leaves, confused children and bewildered goats.

Every soldier in the Visayan scout battalion was taking his family with him to his new post, and from all appearances there was none who had failed to make considerable progress as an ancestor. Children were everywhere.

Babies less than a week old straddled their mothers' hips, girls of six watched their younger brothers and kept them from falling overboard, little tots tumbled about among the piles of baggage, or curled up in quiet corners and slept under life-boats or on coils of rope. Strangely enough, in all the din and hubbub, one thing was absent, the crying of a child.

On the dock, the rest of the garrison, the entire native barrio and the post band, were giving their friends a send-off. Light opera airs were being played, farewells waved, and parting messages shouted.

On the upper deck the American officers of the departing battalion were in the last garrulous stages of taking leave of those who were to remain. A girl, laden with flowers and presents, was off for Manila after a month at Parang. She was more than pleasing to the eye, and later proved equally so to the ear. Four young bachelors clustered around her, each one trying to take her aside and tell her not to forget something-or-other; but she kept them together, talked to all at once, and left each with something pent up in him which found its expression in the long letter which he wrote that night. Doubtless the first letter was answered, then perhaps a picture post card followed from the States, then a lengthy wait and finally an engraved invitation enclosed in a double envelope. It was always the same and might have been very tragic had not another girl visited Parang in the meanwhile.

When a Filipino is born at sea, he is usually given the name of the boat in which he makes his appearance. Consequently, it was not long before Liscum made his appearance, and Liscumia came with the next visit of the stork. Before we reached Iloilo, three more stowaways were added to the passenger list, then finally we disembarked, the five little mothers carried their babies down the gang plank and walked away as sprightly as ever.

Dry and rainy season rolled by, the fire trees bloomed again, and then at last came the order to go home. There was a *despedida* [farewell] at the club, a final ride in a carromata, hand-shakes and messages at the dock, and then the transport slowly turned its bow toward the mouth of the bay.

Beyond the waving arms and fluttering handkerchiefs, two natives were squatting on the shore, boiling something in an earthenware pot. A thin blue curl rose from their fire, spread itself out, and hung like a filmy vapor in the air. The breeze caught it up and wafted it after us, and I drew a deep breath of its perfume. It was the smell of bamboo smoke. Once you have lived in the East and know its fragrance, it will always set you to thinking, to dreaming of bright skies and sparkling blue water, of tiny boats skimming before the soft monsoon, of thatched roofs nestled among the rustling fronds of palms, of brown skins, strange voices, weird music, siestas and content.

EPILOGUE by William C. Buckner

The reader may wonder if Lieutenant Buckner's peacetime Army service was all play and no work. Certainly the field inspections he described in the following letter which he typed to his mother would qualify as work. But he still had one more exciting voyage to make before ending his first two year tour of duty in the Philippines. It would be motoring, or sailing in an emergency, in his 25 foot boat, the 150 mile trip across the Sulu Sea and back. He assures his mother he will be "perfectly safe".

Cebu, P. I.
April 30, 1912

Dear Mother:

You will no doubt have seen ere this in the Register that we are to return on the transport leaving Manila June 15. This delightful piece of news came as a great surprise to us all, and we were certainly pleased to receive it. As yet, we have received no word whatever as to our new station, but it is most probable that we will attend the maneuvers in southern California before going to any post. There is a possibility of our being sent ultimately to Fort Russell, Wyoming; Fort McPherson, Ga., Fort Snelling, Min., or to Plattsburg Barracks, N.Y. McPherson seems to be our most probable destination. The uncertainty of the Mexican situation will probably keep us at "maneuvers" on the border for some time.

For the last three weeks we have been kept moving every moment during our field inspection. The new field inspections are very interesting. The regiments are taken out in full field equipment two or three days' march from their posts. The inspector gives tactical and strategic problems to be solved, tests officers in their ability to make maps and reports, critically examines every organization in signaling, range finding, first aid to the injured, mapping, camp sanitation, field cooking, care of equipment, and animals, care of their feet while on the march, and everything also connected with field service.

The field inspection over, the inspector gave us our garrison inspection, which was an examination in drill, paper work, company administration, and everything relating to our garrison life. Although we have not yet seen the inspector's report, I believe that the regiment showed up very well under test.

I have not yet applied for my leave, on account of the possibility of our being sent to the Mexican border, it is delightful to think of the possibility of spending three months with you and Father in the near future. Two years ago today we were just coming in sight of the Philippines.

The book which you sent me has just arrived and I will read it on the transport going home. I have heard a great deal about it, and it is certainly thoughtful of you to have sent it.

I am about to take a ten day hunting trip to Mindinao. I will leave in about four days and with one civilian and my crew, Isiong, will set sail in the Mermaid. I have lowered the canopy of the boat and put in a bamboo mast and sail to be used in case of emergency, so that trip will be perfectly safe. Dapitan, where we will land, is not more than 150 miles from Cebu. I am looking forward to a very pleasant trip.

With best of love and many thoughts of our happy reunion, I am,

Affectionately,

[Signed] *Bolivar*

Lieutenant Buckner spent a second tour in the Philippines from 1915 through most of 1917. Amidst this tour he sailed home to Louisville, Kentucky, to marry Miss Adèle Blanc to whom he was engaged. She was the daughter of a prominent New Orleans physician. But she was also being pursued by another gentlemen who had the advantage of being nearer. Miss Blanc had wired Buckner a telegram which was meant to say, "DO NOT SAIL", but actually it read, "DO NOT SUIT". Without disclosing this message to his well-wishing friends at the dock, Buckner travelled to Louisville where he socialized with his many friends there until his leave appeared to be over. But he had extended his leave, and he finally got serious with Adèle. She said, "Yes", and on December 30th, 1916, the couple were married by the Episcopal Bishop of Kentucky. The newlyweds honeymooned in the Philippines.

Three months later, April 6th, 1917, when the U.S. declared war on Germany, Buckner expected Theodore Roosevelt would enlist volunteers as he had done during the Spanish American War, so on April 7th he sent the following letter to Colonel Roosevelt. Below is a typed copy of the penciled draft which he kept:

Col Theodore Roosevelt,
Oyster Bay, N.Y.
My dear Col Roosevelt,

The fact of our having declared war yesterday against Germany is very naturally followed by the thought that you will again be on the firing line at the head of a volunteer force.

I still recall with gratitude that I received my appointment to the Military Academy from you, and hope that it will now be my privilege to serve under your command against the enemy. My military record in the War Department is subject to your examination.

My present rank is 1st Lieutenant in the 27th Infantry, having just passed my examination for promotion to captaincy.

Very respectfully,   *[1st Lt. Simon Bolivar Buckner, Jr., Inf., U. S. Army]*

The reply he got from Col. Roosevelt read, "You were down on my list, but the president will not send me", so Buckner transferred to the Air Service department of the Army Signal Corps - probably in hopes this transfer would get him out of the Philippines and into combat. But it was not until in November of 1917 that he even got back to the States. He soloed in a "Jenny" biplane at Kelly Field, Texas, but was told his eyes were not good enough to be a pilot. (His annual physical at that time stated he had 20/40 vision.) But he was sorely needed to train incoming Signal Corps recruits and was retained in that job despite transferring back to his beloved Infantry Branch. In September of 1918 he at last joined an infantry regiment, but his duty was to assist demobilization. The Regular Army was then reduced to a mere 120,000 troops, and for the next 17 years Buckner had no troop duty. Instead, he was either a student or a teacher at Army schools. Eight of those years were at West Point – three of them as Commandant of Cadets.

In 1940 he was promoted to the rank of brigadier general and sent to Alaska to "fortify and defend" that territory. In June of 1942 the Japanese bombed Dutch Harbor in Alaska's Aleutian Islands. The Japanese then occupied the two islands, Attu and Kiska in the far west of that island chain. The joint command of General Buckner and Admiral Thomas Kinkaid drove the Japanese from that United States soil in 1943. For this service Buckner was awarded the Army's Distinguished Service Medal.

In 1944 Buckner was sent to Hawaii to organize the 10th U.S. Army which would land on Okinawa April 1st, 1945. On Okinawa the Japanese fought fiercely from more than 60 miles of underground fortifications. Buckner characterized this battle as "prairie dog warfare". Against it he employed the "blowtorch and corkscrew" tactics of intense naval, air, tank and artillery bombardment of enemy positions followed by Army and Marine ground troops carrying shoulder weapons, grenades and satchel charges. This "typhoon of steel" bombardment and ground attack inflicted lopsided losses on the Japanese who lost 14.9 men killed for every Army or Marine soldier that was killed. Officially the figures were 110,071 Japanese killed vs. 7,374 Americans. Not included in these ground war figures were the 4,907 Navy personnel lost at sea - mostly from Kamikaze attacks.

On June 18th, 1945, three days before the end of organized resistance on Okinawa, General Buckner was up front observing the attack by a newly committed Marine regiment when a Japanese artillery shell hit near him. Though fatally wounded, he rose and asked if anyone else was hurt. When told none, he died with a smile on his face, according to his aide. Posthumously he was awarded the Army's Distinguished Service Cross, his second Army Distinguished Service Medal, the Navy Distinguished Service Medal, the Purple Heart, and the rank of General (four stars). He was the highest ranking American killed by enemy fire in World War II.

Below - 19.5x22 inch copy by Ansel Adams of the Edwin Chapman's portrait of Lt. Gen. Simon Bolivar Buckner Jr. painted in Hawaii in 1944.